REGIONALISM AND UNEVEN DEVELOPMENT IN SOUTHERN AFRICA

Readers seeking an innovative perspective on regionalism in southern Africa, combined with fresh data, could do no better than read Regionalism and Uneven Development in Southern Africa. *No other book so skillfully uncovers regionalizing processes as they relate to neoliberal trends in the subcontinent.*

Professor James H. Mittelman, American University, Washington, USA

The new regionalism is a multifaceted phenomenon, still largely underresearched. This study provides an invaluable, empirically grounded, analysis of the formation of cross-border regionalization in Africa.

Professor Björn Hettne, Göteborg University, Sweden

The Making of Modern Africa

Series Editors: Abebe Zegeye and John Higginson

Wages and Employment in Africa
Dipak Mazumdar with Ata Mazaheri

Globalization and Emerging Trends in African States' Foreign Policy-Making Process
A Comparative Perspective of Southern Africa
Edited by Korwa Gombe Adar and Rok Ajulu

The State, Education and Equity in Post-Apartheid South Africa
The Impact of State Policies
Edited by Enver Motala and John Pampallis

Ecology, Civil Society and the Informal Economy in North West Tanzania
Charles David Smith

Ghana in Search of Development
The Challenge of Governance, Economic Management and Institution Building
Dan-Bright S. Dzorgbo

From Dictatorship to Democracy
Economic Policy in Malawi 1964-2000
Jane Harrigan

Manoeuvering in an Environment of Uncertainty
Structural Change and Social Action in Sub-Saharan Africa
Edited by Boel Berner and Per Trulsson

Gender, Family and Work in Tanzania
Edited by Colin Creighton and C.K Omari

Contesting Forestry in West Africa
Edited by Reginald Cline-Cole and Clare Madge

Regionalism and Uneven Development in Southern Africa

The Case of the Maputo Development Corridor

Edited by

FREDRIK SÖDERBAUM

Göteborg University, Göteborg, Sweden

United Nations University/Comparative Regional Integration Studies (UNU/CRIS), Bruges, Belgium

IAN TAYLOR

University of Botswana, Gaborone, Botswana

University of Stellenbosch, Stellenbosch, South Africa

Routledge

Taylor & Francis Group

LONDON AND NEW YORK

First published 2003 by Ashgate Publishing

Reissued 2018 by Routledge
2 Park Square, Milton Park, Abingdon, Oxon OX14 4RN
711 Third Avenue, New York, NY 10017, USA

Routledge is an imprint of the Taylor & Francis Group, an informa business

A Library of Congress record exists under LC control number: 2003056043

ISBN 13: 978-1-138-71549-3 (hbk)
ISBN 13: 978-1-315-19751-7 (ebk)

Contents

Notes on the Contributors

David Arkwright has occupied various positions in government, local authority and the private sector in both South Africa and Zimbabwe. Whilst employed by the Development Bank of Southern Africa, he played a leading role in conceptualizing the Maputo Development Corridor idea, from which was born the SDI programme. In 1997 he was appointed head of the Maputo Corridor Company and in this capacity played a leading role in facilitating the implementation of initial and subsequent investment projects. Arkwright is now an independent development consultant, advising governments in the southern African region on development issues and on matters relating to development corridors.

Iraê Baptista-Lundin is a social anthropologist and political geographer. She lectured for seven years (1984-91) at Eduardo Mondlane University in Maputo and for seven years (1991-98) as an advisor to the Minister of State Administration in Mozambique. At present she is the Head of the Department of Socio-Political and Cultural Studies at the Centre for Strategic and International Studies (CEEI) of the Higher Institute for International Relations (ISRI) in Maputo.

Admos Chimhowu lectures at the Department of Rural and Urban Planning, University of Zimbabwe. Previously he worked as a senior consultant in the Policy and Strategic Studies Division at the Zimbabwe Institute of Public Administration and Management and as an Environment Research Officer for the non-government organisation ENDA-Zimbabwe. He is also a Leadership for Environment and Development (LEAD) Fellow.

Geoff de Beer is a consulting development planner based in Johannesburg, South Africa. He is the principal of the firm DB Consulting and works extensively throughout southern Africa in areas such as regional economic development (particularly development corridors), tourism-related projects, and the structuring of community/private and community/public/private partnerships. De Beer had extensive involvement in the design of SDI policy and strategy and worked extensively in a consulting capacity on many of the southern African regional development corridors and SDIs, including the Maputo Development Corridor, the TransAfrica Coast-to-Coast, the Nacala Development Corridor, the Swaziland/South Africa Tourism and Biodiversity Corridor, and the Phalaborwa SDI.

James Hentz holds a doctorate from the University of Pennsylvania. He is currently an associate professor at the Virginia Military Institute and has taught at the University of Pennsylvania and Dartmouth College. In 1993/4 he was a visiting scholar at Rand Afrikaans University, Johannesburg, and in 2003 a Fulbright Scholar at Miklós Zrínyi National Defence University, Budapest. He has contributed numerous articles to journals and edited volumes and is co-editor of *New and Critical Security and Regionalism: Beyond the Nation State* (2003). His book, *South Africa and the Logic of Co-operation in Southern Africa* is forthcoming, to be published by Indiana University Press.

Xenia Ngwenya holds an MA in International Studies from the University of Stellenbosch. She has lectured in International Politics and African Politics at the University of South Africa. Her masters' thesis was on the Economic Commission for Africa.

Fredrik Söderbaum is a post-doctoral research fellow at the Department of Peace and Development Research (Padrigu) at Göteborg University and associate research fellow at the United Nations University/Comparative Regional Integration Studies (UNU/CRIS) in Bruges, Belgium. Recent books are *Regionalization in a Globalizing World* (co-edited with M. Schulz and J. Öjendal, 2001); *Theories of New Regionalism* (co-edited with T. Shaw); and *The New Regionalism in Africa* (co-edited with A. Grant).

Ian Taylor holds a MPhil from the University of Hong Kong and a DPhil from the University of Stellenbosch, South Africa. He is currently a lecturer in African politics and International Relations in the Department of Political and Administrative Studies, University of Botswana, as well being a research fellow at the University of Stellenbosch. He has published numerous academic articles and is the author of *Stuck in Middle GEAR: South Africa's Post-Apartheid Foreign Relations* (2001), as well as being a co-editor (with P. Nel and J. van der Westhuizen) of *South Africa's Multilateral Diplomacy and Global Change: The Limits of Reform* (2001).

Daniel Tevera is an associate professor of Human Geography at the University of Zimbabwe. He has published widely on development issues in southern Africa and co-edited (with S. Moyo) *Environmental Security in Southern Africa* (2000) and (with L. Zinyama and S. Cumming) *Harare: the Growth and Problems of the City* (1993).

Acknowledgements

This book has its origins in a research and policy project on industrial policies and corridors co-ordinated by the Development Research Policy Unit (DPRU) at the University of Cape Town during 2000 and 2001. The intriguing discussions held during this project were invaluable and inspired us to put together this book. The financial support from DPRU for the editors' field trips are gratefully acknowledged. The financial and institutional support that made this project possible also included generous research funding from the Swedish International Development Co-operation Agency (Sida), a travel grant from the Nordic Africa Institute, and institutional support from the United Nations University/Comparative Regional Integration Studies (UNU/CRIS).

We are deeply indebted to the two reviewers, James Sidaway and Patrik Stålgren, for invaluable and very constructive comments. We are also grateful to Björn Hettne who has commented on parts of the manuscript. Our very special thanks go to Martin Arvidsson for reading and commenting on the whole manuscript. Thanks also to Eveline Snauwert for her assistance. Needless to say, all faults and errors remain our own.

Finally we would like to thank Kirstin Howgate and Irene Poulton at Ashgate for their encouragement, support as well as patience with us in the completion of this volume.

Fredrik Söderbaum and Ian Taylor, April 2003

Abbreviations

ADB	African Development Bank
ANC	African National Congress
ASSOTSI	Association of the Workers in the Informal Sector
AU	African Union
BIP	Beluluane Industrial Park
BOT	Build-Operate-Transfer
BSAC	British South Africa Company
CEO	Chief Executive Officer
CFM	*Portus e Caminhos de Ferro de Mozambique* (Mozambican Ports and Railway Company)
COMESA	Common Market for Eastern and Southern Africa
CONSAS	Constellation of Southern African States
COSATU	Congress of South African Trade Unions
CPI	Investment Promotion Centre of Mozambique
CSIR	Council for Scientific and Industrial Research
DBSA	Development Bank of Southern Africa
DFID	Department for International Development (UK)
DOT	Department of Transport
DPRU	Development Policy Research Unit
DRC	Democratic Republic of Congo
DTI	Department of Trade and Industry (RSA)
ECA	United Nations Economic Commission for Africa
ECOSOC	United Nations Economic and Social Council
EOI	Export Oriented Industrialisation
EPZ	Export Processing Zone
EU	European Union
FDI	Foreign Direct Investment
Frelimo	*Frente de Libertação de Moçambique*
FTA	Free Trade Area
GATT	General Agreement on Tariffs and Trade
GDP	Gross Domestic Product
GEAR	Growth, Employment and Redistribution

GKG	Gaza-Kruger-Gonarezhou Trans-frontier Park
GNP	Gross National Product
GPZ	Bureau for the Coordination of Development Corridors
IA	Implementing Authority
IDC	Industrial Development Corporation of South Africa
IDZ	Industrial Development Zone
IFC	International Finance Corporation
IFI	international financial institution
IMF	International Metalworkers Federation
IMF	International Monetary Fund
ISI	Import Substitution Industrialisation
ISP	Industrial Strategy Project
ISRI	*Instituto Superior de Relações Internacionals*
LED	Local Economic Development
MCC	Maputo Corridor Company
MCDT	Mozal Community Development Trust
MDC	Maputo Development Corridor
MDHC	Merseyside Docks & Harbour Company
MII	Mpumalanga Investment Initiative
MISP	Maputo Iron and Steel Project
MOZAL	Mozambique Aluminium Smelter
MPDC	Maputo Port Development Company
NEM	Normative Economic Programme
NEPAD	New Partnership for Africa's Development
NGO	Non-Governmental Organisation
NIC	Newly Industrialised Countries
NRA	New Regionalism Approach
NUMSA	National Union of Metal Workers of South Africa
OAU	Organisation of African Unity
OSDICC	Overall SDI Co-ordinating Committee
OTM	Organisation of Mozambican Workers
PARPA/PRSP	*Programa de Acção para a Redução da Pobreza Absoluta*/Poverty Reduction Strategy Paper
PES	*Plano Económico e Social*
PPP	Public-Private Partnership
PRE	*Programa de Reabilitação Nacional*
PTC	Mpumalanga MDC Provincial Technical Committee
RDP	Reconstruction and Development Programme

Renamo	*Resistência Nacional de Moçambique*
RESDIC	Regional SDI Committee
RSA	Republic of South Africa
SACOB	South African Chamber of Business
SACU	Southern African Customs Union
SADC	Southern Africa Development Community
SADCC	Southern African Development Co-ordination Conference
SAP	Structural Adjustment Programme
SARA	Southern African Railway Association
SATCC	Southern African Transport and Communication Commission
SDI	Spatial Development Initiative
SEATOC	South East Africa Tourism Committee
SEMP	Strategic Environmental Management Plan
SINTIME	National Union of Metal and Energy Workers
SMME	Small, Micro and Medium Scale Enterprise
TNC	Transnational Corporation
TRAC	TransAfrica Concessions
UNDP	United Nations Development Programme
UNIDO	United Nations Industrial Development Organisation
UNU/WIDER	United Nations University/World Institute for Development Economics Research
WNLA	Witwatersrand Native Labour Association
WTO	World Trade Organisation

Chapter 1

Introduction: Understanding the Dynamics of Micro-regionalism in Southern Africa

Fredrik Söderbaum and Ian Taylor

The Maputo Development Corridor (MDC) forms part of a larger process of micro-regionalism occurring all over the world. Though the formation of micro-regions is by no means new phenomenon, in the context of globalisation and regionalisation they are increasingly often cross-border in nature rather than contained within the boundaries of a particular nation-state, the conventional understanding of a micro-region. There are many examples of such cross-border micro-regions, for instance, the Euro-regions in Europe, the "Tex-Mex" cross-border region in North America, and the growth triangles in Southeast Asia (Breslin and Hook, 2002; Keating and Loughlin, 1997; Perkmann and Sum, 2002).

The African continent is also filled with a multitude of micro-regions, due to, among other things, the permeability of national borders and the "surface nature" of most nation-state projects on the continent. These micro-regions, or "Afro-regions", appear in various guises: they might be sub-national or cross-border; formal or informal; "real"/cultural or policy-driven and so forth. Since the mid-1990s the so-called Spatial Development Initiatives (SDIs) and development corridors have emerged as the most distinct and probably also the most interesting form of policy-driven micro-regionalism in South and southern Africa.

This volume focuses on the most high profile of all the SDIs, the Maputo Development Corridor (MDC), which is marketed as the "flagship" of the SDI programme. The MDC project is based on a vision to revitalise the axis between the economic heartland of South Africa in Gauteng, South Africa's Mpumalanga province and the city and port of Maputo in Mozambique.

Areas identified by the SDI programme (and this includes the MDC) are those with unrealised economic potential due to a range of historical and political reasons, primarily due to the legacy of apartheid (Jourdan, 1998: 718). A key component of the SDI paradigm is to move away from the protected and isolated import-substitution approach of the past towards one guided rather by international competitiveness, regional co-operation and a more diversified ownership.

The SDIs purport to be short-term and targeted attempts to stimulate economic "growth" by creating globally competitive spatial entities through new investment, infrastructural development and job creation. Through these grand initiatives the state seeks to "crowd in" private investment in order to, so the official discourse goes, unlock inherent economic potential in a specific spatial location. The basic task is to use existing regional frameworks and/or construct new ones as a means to formulate a certain geographic space by which the existing economies can be developed and diversified. In this way the SDI programme is expected to contribute to other key policy areas such as international competitiveness and the wider regional economic integration project as advanced by the Southern African Development Community (SADC). This can be seen as a regional version of the "competition state" through which spaces seek to participate in the liberalised global economy (Cerny, 1997).

Thus, the SDIs programme is explicitly connected to perceptions that in an era marked by globalisation, liberal forms of macro- and micro-regionalisation are a crucial means by which states may come together and tap into the globalisation process in order to maximise their pulling power with regard to international capital. Though part of a wider regional and global process, the SDIs in general and the MDC in particular can thus be seen as concerted attempts by state-society elites to reconstitute micro-regional spaces along lines favoured by private enterprise, particularly externally-oriented fractions of capital, with an eye to the global market.

This particular vision is shared by both the South African and Mozambican governments, who currently see as their primary task the need to work with private capital in close partnership, seeking to facilitate the construction of SDIs such as the MDC: 'the principal mechanism underpinning the SDI programme is private sector investment which will be "crowded in" through a number of public sector interventions' (Lewis and Bloch, 1998: 730). This approach to development and the importance attached to the private sector, is very much in line with the Growth, Employment and Redistribution (GEAR) strategy adopted by the African National Congress (ANC) in South Africa in 1996 (Bond, 2000; Marais, 1998; Taylor, 2001; Williams and Taylor, 2000). In fact, the SDIs have been sold as 'the practical implementation of the government's economic strategy as set out in its Growth, Employment and Redistribution policy' (www.sdi.org.za). Likewise, the SDI approach shares similar conceptions regarding economic growth as the project in Mozambique currently being pursued by the *Frente de Libertação de Moçambique* (Frelimo) government, with much applause from the international financial institutions (IFIs) (Hanlon, 1991, 1996; Abrahamsson and Nilsson, 1995).

The implications of the above is that it is important to situate the MDC within the wider national, regional and global context within which their promoters find themselves. Indeed, the MDC project may be seen as part of a larger phenomenon whereby countries and regions are opening themselves up to the global political economy in a strategy predicated on the gamble that by locking into the globalised world, benefits will surely accrue. The elites within the region most certainly share this view. Swaziland's Economic Planning Minister, Themba Masuku, has remarked on the MDC, that 'there is no question the trade corridor must succeed.

The world is globalising rapidly and regional co-operation is vital if [we] are to cope with increasing competition for trade and investment in the fast-improving world' (quoted in *Sunday Independent*, Johannesburg, 6 November 1996). How this process and the policies enacted at the micro-regional level impact upon the people of the MDC in this 'fast-improving world' remains unspoken and something which this book aims to answer.

This volume complements and advances recent studies on Mozambique and South Africa's development in the era of globalisation and the "post-Washington consensus". One problem with the considerable number of studies on southern Africa is that such analyses are in the main state-oriented and concentrate on national developments. This volume aims to be an advance on this situation as it draws in regional and cross-border issues and processes, situating the micro-region within the wider regional and global political economy. Furthermore, there exist many studies of regionalism in Africa and southern Africa, both old and more recent. In general, however, this past research is mainly focused on macro-regions and inter-state frameworks, such as SADC, the Common Market for Eastern and Southern African (COMESA), the Organisation of African Unity (OAU) and so forth. It is difficult to dispute that state-centrism was a major flaw of old regionalism studies. In contrast, some of the more important "new regionalism" studies have moved away from simple state-based ontologies, taking into account processes within and across communities, ecological and gender perspectives, and the multifaceted relationship between globalisation and regional projects (cf. Bach, 1999; Hettne et al., 1999; Poku, 2001; Simon, 1998; Söderbaum, 2002; Söderbaum and Shaw, 2003). Valuable as they are in helping us understand the regionalising impulses underway, there are however very few in-depth case studies on how such regionalisms are affecting people "on the ground" and within specified micro-regional contexts (for an exception see Grant and Söderbaum, 2003). It is our conviction that focusing on micro-level regional processes—on micro-regions themselves—helps overcome this difficulty.

The neglect of micro-regionalism in the study of international studies is unfortunate, since it is perhaps the form of regionalism most beholden to "real" processes on the ground. In this sense, micro-regions are most obviously constructed at the interface between the top-down and the bottom-up, and with very "real" implications for people living in the area. Frequently, top-down activities merely grant state legitimacy over processes that have long-existed and that are least obligated to what administrations may or may not pursue. Concrete studies of micro-regional interactions is perhaps the most fruitful in lifting the veil of obscurity over much of what is "really" occurring and identifying the interface between elite-derived agendas and popular reactions to such processes.

This introductory chapter seeks to do the following. The next two sections describe the historical background to the formation of the MDC and the stated objectives and major projects of the MDC respectively. The third section outlines the purpose of this book. The fourth rather comprehensive section discusses and defines the overall theoretical framework guiding the analysis in the volume, namely the new regionalism approach (NRA). Finally, the structure of the book is described.

Genealogy of the Maputo Development Corridor

The MDC was launched in May 1996 by the Presidents of Mozambique and South Africa. The process however began in August 1995 when the Ministers of Transport of Mozambique and South Africa, Mac Maharaj and Paulo Muxanga respectively, met to set in motion a plan to establish a developmental axis between the port of Maputo and the industrial centre of South Africa (Gauteng). This process can be seen very much as an attempt to reconstruct a cross-border relationship and micro-region that had effectively existed since at least the industrialisation of the area around present-day Johannesburg since the late 1800s.

Indeed, the geographical area pointing up north from the eastern part of South Africa to Mozambique and Swaziland has constituted a historical regional space (with the Maputo corridor as one core) for the people of southeastern Africa for centuries (McGregor, 1994). Since ancient times there has existed a migratory and trading tradition through and across this geographic space. With the brutal incorporation of the peoples of this micro-region into capitalist colonial economies, many of these long-standing patterns were formalised by the Europeans as a means of control. After the so-called pacification campaign carried out by Portugal in Mozambique in 1895, an accord was signed to regulate the influx of labour to the mines in the Transvaal in 1897. This arrangement allowed White South African capital to exploit Black Mozambican labour through various agreements with the metropole, often against the wishes of the local Portuguese. Such arrangements made Mozambique a regional conduit and effective labour reserve for the minerals-based industries in South Africa (Smith, 1991). This process not only locked southern Mozambique and the Johannesburg environs together, it served to crystallise an already nascent micro-region. Indeed, the 1903 agreement between the Portuguese colonial power and the Witwatersrand Native Labour Association (WNLA), the representative grouping of the great South African mining houses, firmly established the migratory labour system that formed/forms the basis of the historical space around which the MDC has been formulated (Katzenellenbogen, 1982). Importantly, the agreement gave the WNLA exclusive rights to recruit Black labour in southern Mozambique in return for directing 47.5 per cent of the export traffic from the Witwatersrand through the port at Lourenço Marques (now Maputo) (Mondlane, 1969: 93). This meant that a transport corridor linking Johannesburg and its environs to the Indian Ocean—and the world—through Maputo port developed and became a major feature of southern Africa's regional dynamics, accounting for much of the development of Maputo (Penvenne, 1995). Being the shortest link to an export harbour for South Africa's industrial heartland, this corridor also rapidly became a major intersection for southern Africa's linkages with the world economy: by the 1970s, 40 per cent of exports from the Witwatersrand area went through Maputo (DBSA, 2001a). Going in the opposite direction, hundreds of thousands of Mozambicans travelled to work as migrant labourers in the minerals industries along the Witwatersrand, as well as others finding work as agricultural contract workers (Niemann, 1998: 9). Between 1908 and 1975 the annual flow of legally recruited labourers from Mozambique fluctuated between 74,000 and 118,000 (Mamdani, 1996: 153), and by 1994, over

150,000 of the more than 250,000 workers in Gauteng's gold mines came from outside of South Africa (Crush, 1997: 20). Thus, it should be clear that migration was a crucial component of this special and asymmetric corridor (see Baptista-Lundin and Taylor, chapter 8).

Contextualising this, Portuguese East Africa developed into a series of transport corridors: to Southern Rhodesia (Beira), to Nyasaland, across Tete in the north and to South Africa (Lourenço Marques), etc. After independence the new Mozambican government put in place a planning apparatus designed to foster national territorial integration, for instance upgrading the North-South highway. This however was thwarted by the civil war with Renamo and South African sabotage. The MDC and corridor strategies in general can thus be seen as a revitalisation of past development strategies advanced by Maputo (Sidaway, 1993).

This being so, the historical corridor is larger than just Maputo as an end-station. Agricultural products have long been brought in from other parts of Mozambique and sold in Maputo, and revenues are used to buy goods in South Africa and Swaziland and other neighbouring countries, to be sold back in Maputo (see Baptista-Lundin and Taylor, chapter 8; Van den Berg, 1987). This movement and trading has created a never-ending cycle of new types of business, hawking, trading and interaction, increasing the flow of people along the corridor. In this way Maputo attracts people from all over Mozambique and neighbouring countries, with many people staying on in Maputo to join the increasingly informal market, often connected to a regularly or daily crossing of borders to buy products for sale, both in Maputo and further afield. Various attempts have been made to regulate and control borders, smuggling, informal trading, hawking and migration, but people have often found other ways to get around these restrictions. In fact, the insurgency by Renamo simply intensified and opened up further space for informal cross-border linkages and trading networks, which centred around Maputo but at the same time permeated the whole micro-region (McGregor, 1998).

This cross-border interaction has been further intensified by another important trend that emerged when the socialist experience was abandoned in Mozambique and the old safety net provided by the state gradually disappeared (Simpson, 1993; Abrahamsson and Nilsson, 1995). Despite attempts (albeit erratically) to provide some form of economic incentives to agriculture (Cravinho, 1998), many people left this traditional occupation and entered the market sector, mostly in the cities (Kyle, 1991). In 1990 commerce had already surpassed agriculture as the main occupation for women in Maputo (Little and Lundin, 1993: 1-8). The informal market expanded to all corners of the country as well as linking up with neighbouring countries, marking the beginning of the institution of *mukhero*, a largely informal movement of people, mostly women, buying and transporting all types of goods, vegetables, fruits, clothes and small home appliances, between Mozambique and South Africa and Swaziland, to buy products to sell on the informal market (Baptista-Lundin and Taylor, chapter 8). Initially it was mainly a question of acquiring agricultural products to supply a market in need, because the situation of war had cut the roads to Maputo from the countryside. Later on, other products were incorporated into the *mukhero*. To a large extent the *mukhero* represent modern survival strategies, but several of the women traders have also constructed viable business enterprises.

In summary, it was upon such historically rooted and extensive cross-border (if informal) initiatives that the MDC sought to build upon, in a wider attempt to restructure the micro-region along certain, more guided, lines.

The MDC: Stated Objectives and Major Projects

The MDC is based on four key objectives:

1. To rehabilitate the primary infrastructure network along the corridor, notably road, rail, port and dredging, and border posts, with the participation of the private sector in order to have minimum impact on the fiscus.
2. To maximise investment in both the inherent potential of the corridor area and in the added opportunities which infrastructure rehabilitation will create, including the provision of access to global capital and facilitation of regional economic integration.
3. To maximise social development, employment opportunities and increase the participation of historically disadvantaged communities; and
4. To ensure sustainability by developing policy, strategies and frameworks that ensure a holistic, participatory and environmentally sustainable approach to development.

The basic idea behind the MDC initiative is the implementation of a large number of investment projects, of which the most important are the "mega-projects" (see De Beer and Arkwright, chapter 2). The architects of the MDC identified, designed and packaged various investment projects, which were then presented at an investors' conference in May 1996. This conference marked the official launch of the MDC, at which no less than 180 project proposals were presented to investors, with a value of nearly US$7 billion and with the stated potential to generate up to 35,000 jobs. In other words, the MDC contained a very comprehensive investment portfolio. A rough distinction can be made between infrastructural projects and the major economic development projects. With regard to the rehabilitation of primary infrastructure, the following projects, with a total estimated value of US$661.5 million, were of crucial importance. Firstly, the Witbank-Maputo N4 toll road. This was the first major Public-Private Partnership (PPP) in southern Africa and was concessioned for 30 years to a private sector consortium, TransAfrica Concessions (TRAC), on the basis of "build, operate and transfer" (BOT) (see Ngwenya and Taylor, chapter 6). Other projects included the rehabilitation of the port of Maputo; the establishment of a public/private company to manage, operate and maintain the southern Mozambique rail network; and a single facility/one-stop border post at Ressano Garcia/Komatipoort.

The most comprehensive economic development projects were the US$1.3 billion Mozambique Aluminium Smelter (Mozal), which in the second phase was supplemented, making it worth a total of more than US$2 billion in investment (see

Hentz, chapter 7). The Maputo Iron and Steel Project (US$1.5 billion) and the Beluluane Industrial Park (BIP), which is an industrial free zone aiming to attract foreign, regional and local investment to heavy industry manufacturing and hi-tech industries, were also key projects, as was the Pande/Temane gas pipeline (US$250 million). In addition to these gigantic projects there were a significant number of other investment projects, in fields such as: mining (a magnetite, vanadium and heavy minerals project), energy, chemicals, manufacturing, agriculture, forestry, commerce and tourism (eco-tourism, lodge and game-park development and so on see De Beer and Arkwright, chapter 2).

Furthermore, subsequent policy-makers developed MDC technical support programmes in order to complement the projects mentioned above (first and foremost in order to achieve MDC objective 3 and 4). Some of the most important support programmes included the cluster and linkage processes; policy research and capacity building; strategic environmental management plan (SEMP); local economic development (LED); and institution building.

Objectives of the Book

This volume aims to examine the formal/informal, governmental, developmental and societal features of the MDC that seem most vital for any micro-regional construction. As emphasised above, there is a special emphasis on how local communities regard and respond to the MDC initiative "on the ground". Whilst informal "on the ground" analysis is central, this volume centres around the two closely related dimensions of micro-regionalism that straddle the formal/informal nexus: governance and development. Essentially, the thrust of this book is to answer key questions such as: who decides what and with what means in the MDC (i.e. the governance factor) and for whom, for what purpose and with what consequences is the MDC implemented (i.e. the development factor).

In the literature there is a tendency to focus on either governance *or* development, which seems to be explained by the disciplinary divide between political science and economics. This volume seeks to bridge this gap and by doing so contribute to interdisciplinary inquiries and a broader research agenda associated with regional development projects in Africa. It is in this sense very much influenced by International Political Economy (IPE).

The relationship between governance and development is both multifaceted and symbiotic. Indeed, the MDC represents an interesting form of cross-border governance that needs to be analysed in order to expand our understanding of multilevel and transnational governance. This in turn further contributes to the study of development within a transnational context, a most meaningful task in the current epoch of a rapidly globalising and regionalising world.

Seen from the development side of the equation, it is apparent that although the SDIs correspond to familiar developmental strategies around "growth poles", a significant feature is the ambition to foster the "right conditions" for investment projects and PPPs as instruments for economic growth. Development is presumed to be a spin-off from such scenarios. This strategy of "pull-growth" (as opposed to "push-growth") is very much dependent on the particular form of governance within the SDIs. Governance is thus intimately related to development within the SDI methodology. In fact, governance can be seen as the precondition for development. Seen in this way, development can perhaps be seen as the main test of effective governance.

Although there is a crucial and much neglected relationship between governance and development, which this volume seeks to explore, it is still fruitful to raise some detailed research questions with regard specifically to each of these two phenomena. Starting with governance, the planning, resolution and execution of the MDC are based on a special decision-making and implementation procedure, what is often referred to as a generalised "SDI methodology". This formula groups a number of various agents and stakeholders, such as central governments, development finance institutions, provincial and local governments, private businesses, interest groups and local communities together, reflecting what has been seen as a shift from government to governance. Seen from this perspective, one important question is where does power lie in the MDC governance structures and the broader "SDI methodology"? Does power lie with the central governments or with provincial administrations? Where does local government fit in and how is private business and civil society accommodated? Which actors have the most "voice" in the MDC and why? Indeed, what stakeholders are included and what excluded in the rather complex and network-like governance structures that characterise the MDC? To what extent is the stated goal of "local participation" enhanced in the governance structures of the MDC?

It must be admitted that it is somewhat difficult to assess the depth and longevity of "development", given the relatively recent history of the MDC. Nevertheless, this volume does seek to analyse what tangible development effects have arisen as a direct outcome of investment and infrastructural projects within the MDC framework. First of all, it is crucial to assess the nature of the development strategy as such. What does "development" mean in the context of the MDC? What type of development (if any) is actually being introduced? Certainly, it is important to ask in what ways and to what extent have the jobs created in the MDC contributed to empowerment and capacity-building in the local communities? Have other stated goals of the MDC been satisfied, such as new production opportunities for small, micro and medium size businesses? Furthermore, in what ways have the various initiatives associated with the MDC impacted upon issues of gender relations in general and the empowerment of women in particular?

The above points take us back to the central aim of this book, which is to seek to analyse how the MDC has impacted people "on the ground". By looking at a variety of cross-cutting levels of governance and development and by focusing on the intriguing nexus between the formal and informal processes that stake out the MDC, this volume aims to contribute to a detailed understanding of the "flagship" of the SDI programme in southern Africa. Importantly, the MDC has been marketed by both Pretoria and Maputo as a model for future SDIs in southern Africa. Its success or otherwise and the processes engendered by the various projects within the MDC ambit are thus of crucial importance. In consequence, this book will seek to analyse the lessons to be learnt from what has already occurred within the MDC and the policy implications for other such SDIs in southern Africa.

The New Regionalism Approach

A large number of frameworks and theories, both old and new, are available for the study of regionalism. The research field, or at least its research output, is dominated by mainstream and conventional theories of regional co-operation and integration, such as neo-realism, functionalism, neo-functionalism, institutionalism and economic integration theory. There is no doubt that such studies have contributed to the understanding of regionalism and regionalist projects, both in the past as well as for today's regionalism.

However, these frameworks need to be challenged for a number of reasons. One of their weaknesses is that their positivistic logic of investigation results in a concern with the methodology of regionalism rather than a systematic concern for the socio-economic circumstances and historical context in which regionalism occurs. This weakness is closely related to the fact that these theories are developed first and foremost for the study of Europe. When this geographic focus is transcended the main focus is placed on North America and the Asia-Pacific. Even in such "developed" regionalisms, variations from the "norm" are explained in terms of how they differ from the "standard case" of Europe. It is revealing that one of the core contributions to rationalist regionalism, *The Political Economy of Regionalism* (Mansfield and Milner, 1997), "conveniently" ignores Africa and the dynamic regionalisation processes on this continent (also see Adler and Barnett, 1998; Fawcett and Hurrell, 1997; Mattli, 1999). Apart from the narrow empirical selection, the problem lies, generally speaking, in that the same underlying assumptions and conceptualisations—such as the notion of unitary states, the regulating influence of regional organisations, trade and policy-led economic integration and so on—that stem from a particular reading of European integration influence the description and prescription of regionalism in the rest of the world. Such discursive hegemony is maintained by the common accusation that critical and reflective approaches are "non-scientific" and speculative (Mattli, 1999: 3-16). Critical studies are also, it must be said, simply ignored (e.g. by Mansfield and Milner, 1997).

This volume adopts what has become established as the new regionalism approach (NRA). This is by no means a homogeneous school of thought, but the "new regionalisms/new realist approach" refers to a diverse group of relatively like-minded scholars who share important common denominators and interact in overlapping networks of research (e.g. Hettne et al., 1999, 2000a, b, c, 2001; Hettne and Söderbaum, 1998, 2000; Mittelman, 2000; Schulz et al., 2001; Söderbaum, 2002; Bøås et al. 1999). In the broadest sense the "world order approach" associated with the University of Sheffield's Political Economy Research Centre is also rather closely related to the same school of thought (see Gamble and Payne, 1996; Hook and Kearns, 1999; and Breslin and Hook, 2002).

The NRA is connected with a broader theoretical debate within the field of IPE. Somewhat simplified, it is best understood within the broader tradition of critical, reflectivist or "new" IPE and the effort to transcend and challenge "problem-solving" mainstream theories (Murphy and Tooze, 1991; Hettne, 1995; Cox, 1996a). As such, the NRA is founded on the necessity to "unpack" the state, avoiding the exaggerated state-centrism inherent in mainstream theorising in the field—be it neo-realism, institutionalism and/or economic integration theory—and critically assess state-society complexes in the formation of regions. In this way the NRA opens up for a broad and deep interdisciplinary, critical/reflectivist understanding of what characterises regionalism and regionalisation in various parts of the world. As Mittelman points out:

> The new regionalism approach (NRA) is an important advance of the different versions of integration theory (trade or market integration, functionalism and neo-functionalism, institutionalism and neo-institutionalism, and so on)...[A]ll of them are deficient inasmuch as they understate power relations and fail to offer an explanation of structural transformation. In some ways a break with this tradition, the NRA explores contemporary forms of transnational co-operation and cross-border flows through comparative, historical, and multilevel perspectives (Mittelman, 1999: 25-26).

The NRA starts from the proposition that in order to understand regionalism today it is essential to realise that we are dealing with a qualitatively new phenomenon, which is taking place in a new context and with a new content. With regard to context, the new regionalism needs to be related to the current transformation of the world: regions are not formed in a vacuum. Here globalisation is a key to further understanding. Globalisation and regionalisation are intimately connected, and must thus be understood within the same framework, together shaping the emerging world order. 'The new regionalism and multipolarity are, from a world order perspective, two sides of the same coin' (Hettne, 2002: 2). The content of the renewed trend towards regionalism changing the world today has also been altered radically. While the old regionalism was often imposed, directly or indirectly, from above and outside, in accordance with Cold War power structures, the new regionalism often emerges from in accordance with regional peculiarities and problems. As a consequence, the new regionalism is a truly world-wide phenomenon, taking place in more areas of the world than ever before. Furthermore, the old regionalism was generally specific with regard to objectives and content, with a particular focus on free trade arrangements and security alliances, whereas the new is resulting from a more comprehensive and multi-dimensional societal process.

The concept and the content of "region" is fundamental to the study of regionalism. Historically, the concept of region has been defined first and foremost as a space between the "national" and the "local" (municipality), primarily within particular "states". These types of regions are what we refer to as micro-regions. The concept of region can also refer to macro-regions (world regions), which are larger territorially (in contrast with non-territorial) units or subsystem, between the "state" and the "global".

Many (mainstream) disciplines and discourses have maintained a strong emphasis on "territory", "function" and "rule" in the study and definition of regions. Regardless of whether the focus has been on macro-regions or micro-regions, a considerable degree of research capacity has been devoted to determining what "types" of regions are the most functional, instrumental and efficient. Often, especially in Political Science and Economics, regions have been taken as (pre-)given, defined in advance of research, and frequently simply seen as particular interstate frameworks. Integral to this reasoning is that regions are believed to exist "out there", identifiable through material structures and inter-state frameworks.

According to the reflectivist perspective built upon in the NRA, regions are seen as social constructions and social settings created by state and non-state actors for a host of different reasons. From this point of view, the puzzle is to understand and explain the phenomenon of regionalism and the process through which regions are coming into existence and are being consolidated—their "becoming" so to speak—rather than a particular set of activities and flows within a pre-given (and often pre-scientific) region or regional framework. As Neumann (1999: 115) points out, 'the existence of regions is preceded by the existence of region-builders'.

Contrary to the mainstream and problem-solving concern with more or less fixed and static definitions of regions, the NRA is more eclectic and more focused on the processes and consequences of regionalisation in various fields of activity and at various levels. These are the processes through which regions are being made and unmade. The NRA suggests by no means that regions will be unitary, homogeneous or discrete units. Instead there are many varieties of regional subsystems, with different degrees of "regionness" (Hettne, 1993, 1999, 2002; Hettne and Söderbaum, 2000). There are no natural or given regions, but these are constructed, deconstructed and reconstructed—intentionally or unintentionally—in the process of global transformation, by collective human action and identity formation. Regionalism is a heterogeneous, comprehensive, multi-dimensional phenomenon, taking place in several sectors and often pushed by a variety of state, market, society and external actors both within and outside formal regional organisations.

It should be evident that the NRA looks beyond state-centrism. From the perspective of NRA, regionalism is more comprehensive and dynamic than inter-state action. States are not the only regionalising actors, and market, civil society—as well as external actors—are deeply involved in processes of regionalisation, including its political dimensions. Rather than separating actors into perceived "autonomous" groups of actors, the NRA suggests that actors will be grouped in—formal or informal—multi-actor collectivities (networks and modes of governance). It is important to critically assess these new modes of governance and "partnerships" with a focus on by whom, for whom and for what purpose they are being erected.

The NRA stipulates that regionalism will/can be used for the achievement of a wide range of different goals—private as well as public—that can be compatible and mutually reinforcing but also competitive. Regionalism is more complex (and sometimes also more detrimental) than simply being an instrument to enhance an ambiguous "national interest" (realism) or the procurement of the "public good" or "trade" (liberalism). Potentially, state actors create regionalisation in order to achieve private goals and promote particular (vested) interests rather than broader societal interests. As a result, regionalisation will not necessarily be harmonious or beneficial to all participants. On the contrary, under certain circumstances it can be exclusionary, exploitative, and also reinforce asymmetries and imbalances.

An actor's decision to engage in regionalism/regionalisation will depend not only on material incentives and resources (including power capabilities, routine behaviour, or what we might refer to as "economic man") but also on ideas and identities. What regional actors do depend on who they are, their worldviews, who other actors are as well as the quality and quantity of their interactions.

Before moving on it is apposite to make some conceptual clarifications. In its broadest sense, "regionalism" refers to the general phenomenon of regionalism (or simply what we term the "New Regionalism"). In a more narrow and operational sense, regionalism represents the body of ideas, values, and concrete objectives associated with a specific regional project that an identifiable group of actors wish to realise. This is the urge by any set of actors to reorganise along regional lines in any given area. Regionalism in this particular sense is usually associated with a formal programme (and often leads to institution-building). Furthermore, regionalism ties agents to one specific project that is clearly limited spatially or socially but not necessarily in time (Hveem, 2000: 72).

Regionalisation is the actual process of increasing contact, exchange, co-operation and integration within a given region (sometimes referred to as the outcome). Regionalisation may be caused by regionalism, but it may also emerge regardless of whether there is a regionalist project and regionalism ideology or not (Hveem, 2000: 73). In fact, it should be recognised that regionalisation may occur unintentionally, without actors necessarily being conscious of or dedicated to it. Likewise, the rhetoric and ideology of regionalism may not always have much practical significance to the reality of regionalisation. Through the usage of regionalism/regionalisation however, we are able to overcome the somewhat artificial distinction between regional co-operation and regional integration. Too often there is a belief that regional integration is fundamentally different, compared to regional co-operation, and that there even may exist a conflict between them (Christiansen, 2001). In the broadest sense, regional integration is seen as "forming parts into a whole", but in a more concrete sense at least political scientists tend to highlight the establishment of supranational (regional) institutions and their independent activities, for instance the European Commission or the Court. Regional co-operation is more open-ended and less demanding, referring to the fact that actors may co-operate in order to achieve common objectives in one area, in spite of conflicting interests and objectives in another.

Needless to say, it is sometimes fruitful to keep the concepts of "regional integration" and "regional co-operation" distinct. However, through the usage of regionalism and regionalisation the NRA is able to account for the complexity and multidimensionality of current regionalism/regionalisation, involving co-operation and integration among a variety of actors and supported by a diversity of institutional frameworks in both formal and informal settings (see Söderbaum and Shaw, 2003).

Bringing in Micro-regionalism

In the field of IPE the macro-region has been the most common object of analysis. Even though many frameworks in the research field (to some extent also including the NRA) often acknowledge the pluralism of regions, the main concern has been with the macro-regions rather than micro-regions. In our view this has lead to an under-emphasis of the heterogeneity and pluralism of regionalisation as well as micro-issues on the ground. In response, this volume seeks to bridge the rift between macro-regionalism and micro-regionalism, drawing attention to their close relationships rather than their differences. The great pluralism and diversity of regionalisms at different levels implies that in trying to bridge the gap, it is not sufficient to dichotomise them as either "from above" (macro) or "from below" (micro), which is sometimes done. Mittelman (2000: 158) is correct in that '[g]lobalisation has not spawned such ideal types but, rather, a mix of contested sub-regional projects: strategies, in various degrees spontaneous or deliberate, home-grown or emulated. These include different generations or iterations of the NIC model, growth triangles and polygons often encompassing EPZs and development corridors, and transfrontier growth areas'. Sometimes the state has more autonomy from social forces and at other times the global market penetrates more deeply than in others.

As has been noted, so far the critical/reflectivist regionalism literature has not engaged in any rigorous examination of micro-regional processes. What work that does exist, particularly on Africa, is limited to single case studies (e.g. Breslin and Hook, 2002; Grant and Söderbaum, 2003; Söderbaum, 2002). There is thus a serious gap in the literature as studies on micro-regions promises to be an important field of research in most disciplines within the social sciences in the future. Indeed, the study of micro-regions in Europe, the so-called Euro-regions, is a rapidly growing field of research. Similar trends can be witnessed with regard to Asia (Breslin and Hook, 2002; Mittelman, 2000; Perkmann and Sum, 2002). The basic point of departure for this volume is that it is important to recognise the emergence of the same phenomenon in Africa as well.

These micro-regions may or may not fall within the borders of a particular nation-state. Micro-regionalism is often constituted by a network of transactions and collaboration across national boundaries, which may very well emerge as an alternative or in opposition to the challenged state, as well as to formal state regionalisms. However, as illustrated by the concepts of growth polygons, growth triangles, development corridors, spatial development initiatives, cross-border regions etc., micro-regionalism in the South is nevertheless often state-assisted with a weak degree of formal institutionalisation. At the same time they are often private market-driven and involve a high degree of interactions initiated by non-state actors (corporations and NGOs) and inter-personal transnational networks such as diasporas, ethnic or family networks, religious ties, etc. (Perkmann and Sum, 2002; Mittelman, 2000). Furthermore, there is a clear possibility that in the future these micro-regions may increasingly co-ordinate their activities or even integrate. But once again, the relationship between actors and processes at various levels is seldom linear or evolutionary but rather contradictory and disparate.

The NRA, Globalisation and Uneven Development

It is important to consider the external factor in the analysis of various forms of regionalism. The negligence of the global and external factor was often a fallacy of "old" theories of regional integration, particularly functionalism, neo-functionalism and regional economic integration theories, whereas most "new regionalism" theories acknowledge the external dimension and the close relationship between globalisation and regionalisation.

Obviously, no single definition of globalisation can encompass all the various permutations and features associated with this catch-all word across time and space. Indeed, the concept is quite eclectic, describing global economic integration *and* political, social, cultural, ecological and gender-wise outcomes. Yet, we can talk about the making global, as opposed to territory-specific (including regionalisation), of a wide variety of things, both social and economic, implying the widening in scope and deepening of a variety of economic and political (though the two cannot be separated) processes. In essence, globalisation is undermining the distinction between the international and domestic and the external/internal (Held et al., 1999: 7).

It is crucial to understand that there exist many different ways to look upon the relationship between globalisation and regionalisation. The NRA is fundamentally different compared to the parallel discourse of "new" or "open regionalism" among neo-liberal economists and policy-makers in the international financial institutions (IFIs) and the World Trade Organisation (De Melo and Panagaryia, 1993). According to the NRA, globalisation and regionalisation are intimately connected, and must thus be understood within the same framework, together shaping the emerging world order as well as the regions as such (Hettne et al., 1999). The NRA also views (economic) globalisation as a strong and in some of its dimensions irreversible force, with deep implications for regionalism and development. Similar to the open regionalism discourse, the NRA accepts that economic globalisation and many forms of regionalism are mutually reinforcing in the contemporary world. But in sharp contrast to the former, the NRA has a more sceptical and critical attitude of what is happening. The NRA considers many forms of current regionalism to be manifestations of economic globalisation and prevailing forms of hegemony. Viewed from this perspective, both economic globalisation and open regionalism are seen as highly uneven processes which reinforce imbalances between and within countries. The NRA seeks to detect and reveal the power relations driving these grand processes.

Here it is fruitful to relate to policy discussions in the South and in Africa. Although it is possible to talk of a "post-Washington consensus", the dominant political and economic model for the South in general and Africa in particular demands that economies must look outward towards the global market as a means to attract resources and investment. This, so the discourse goes, is best achieved by "openness" through global and regional economic integration. In this light, state administrations must seek to construct and extend free trade areas and encompass more and more territories, whilst at the same time opening up their own economies. The eventual goal is to consolidate and integrate existing free trade areas, whereby borders and protective measures and other "obstacles to free trade" become mere memories. This vision is the basis upon which both SADC and COMESA are currently predicated upon, however far away into the future the realisation of such objectives may be. Eventually, such giant free trade areas would constitute "stepping stones" towards the construction of a single global economy. In other words, as seen from this particular perspective, the goal is to synchronise regional market integration with economic globalisation/multilateralism, through open forms of regionalism.

The SDIs in general and the MDC in particular are intended to bring globalisation to southern Africa at the same time as it enhances (open) economic integration in the region. In this way there is no competition, but rather an anticipated synergy and close association between globalisation as well as various forms of open regionalisms (macro as well as micro) (Söderbaum, 2002).

However, as indicated above, according to the NRA a linear relationship between globalisation and regionalisation is the least likely to occur. Furthermore, much more research attention needs to be devoted to understanding the power relations behind these processes, and their developmental impacts in particular. One of the core problems in this regard is that 'most discussions on globalisation and "development" take for granted the benefits of export orientation and more trade, wondering only if more or less, and what kind of state activity facilitates a positive insertion in the global political economy' (Moore, 1999: 80). But, as pointed out by Gill (1995: 405), 'the [globalisation] concept serves to reify a global economic system dominated by large institutional investors and transnational firms which control the bulk of the world's productive assets and are the principal influences in world trade and financial markets'. 'Transnational capital, in the institutional form of transnational corporations, now disaggregates and disperse production to take advantage of global differentials in labour regimes, labour processes, and industrial organisations, and to maximise profitability' (Yaghmaian, 1998: 249). Importantly, this scenario has created what Hirschman (1981) long ago referred to as 'mono-economics', that is, the belief that there exists a universal set of economic laws that apply across the board and that policy-making is essentially about conforming to such laws. Mittelman (1999: 44) has eloquently pointed out the negative effects of such a paradigm, in regard to development and regionalism:

> Concerned as it is with purportedly universal laws of development, neo-liberal theory posits that, in principle, the same rules of economic development can be applied across the board from the most developed to the least developed countries. As such, the theory is overly mechanical and represents a slot machine approach to regionalism. Taking an individualist approach, it is silent about deep structural

> inequalities, especially the qualitative aspects of underdevelopment lodged in the blockage of highly inegalitarian social systems ... What is more, neo-liberals' vision of a friction-less world of shared meanings, the uncontested adaptation of the ideology of capitalism, is structurally blind to patterns of domination and hegemony.

This draws attention to the fact that due to its origins in critical IPE, one of the purposes of the NRA is the ambition to understand and contribute to structural transformation and social change, with a particular emphasis on the impact and consequence of uneven development and various forms of domination. This focus draws our attention to the content of development rather than the form, implying a critical questioning of what type of development, for whom and with what consequences. In fact, rooted in critical IPE, an unbending concern for the excluded, poor and marginalised is maintained, critically questioning existing structures and in whose interests the prevailing strategies are carried out. Such questions constitute perhaps the most important component of the NRA.

In response to the above, an important component of the NRA is to identify the counter-forces and agents of transformation in the context of economic globalisation. Mittelman (2000: 225) labels this 'transformative regionalism', referring to the alternative and bottom-up forms of cultural identity and regional self-organisation and self-protection, such as pro-democracy forces, women's movements, environmentalists and so on. 'At the end of the day, the possibilities and limitations of transformative regionalism rest on the strength of its links to civil society' (Mittelman, 1999: 48). The hypothesis of this volume is that it is perhaps at the micro-regional level that this is most apparent.

Structure of the Book

The next chapter is written by two of the main architects of the MDC, Geoff de Beer and David Arkwright; the first as a consultant and the latter as the South African project manager. These two authors provide an overview of the progress achieved and lessons learned of the MDC. Their study begins with a summary of the MDC's main objectives, strategies and underlying design principles. Thereafter follows an outline of the main infrastructure and economic development projects and programme-related interventions of the MDC, followed by a brief assessment of the progress achieved with these projects and programmes to date. The authors then move on to highlight a number of key lessons arising from the MDC as well as some of the key strengths and weaknesses of the MDC.

In chapter 3, Daniel Tevera and Admos Chimhowu situates the MDC in a broader regional context. Taking a regional perspective, the authors outline and discusses the MDC within the context of south-eastern Africa as well as the wider southern Africa region. Tevera and Chimhowu begin with the observation that corridors are not new phenomena and that there exists several other (new and old) types of spatial and regional frameworks for development. The authors then go on to briefly discuss the process leading up to the formation of the MDC as well as some of the developmental impacts of the MDC as such. Before concluding, the authors move into the macro-regionalism versus micro-regionalism debate, with a particular focus on the relationship between the MDC and SADC.

In chapter 4, Fredrik Söderbaum and Ian Taylor interrogate the economic development philosophy behind the MDC, problematising the role of the state in this project. Their analysis reveals several flaws in the MDC that reinforces the effective role of the state as a transmission belt for transnational capital rather than as a facilitator for development. For instance, the market fundamentalism and "big-bang" approach inherent in the MDC has spelt "jobless growth" thus far, highly problematic in light of the bold developmental claims made by promoters of the MDC. Similarly, the notion that "good governance is less government", implies that the state is to a large extent reduced to being an "investment promotion agency" rather than having a stabilising role in the political economy. Söderbaum and Taylor are also critical of the implementation and planning processes of the MDC, particularly the fast-track approach with regard to the effect this has on economic development. Having said this, the MDC *does* contain several novel and positive features and the problematic aspects might be overcome through some strategic changes in the MDC approach. The contribution by Söderbaum and Taylor urges a heavier focus on development, a more pro-active state, and more comprehensive and inclusive governance structures.

In chapter 5, Fredrik Söderbaum seeks to assess the specific and interesting modes of governance in the MDC, with a particular focus on who decides what, for whom and with what means? The chapter starts out with mapping the institutional landscape that surrounds the MDC and the particular planning and implementation process of the initiative. Then, Söderbaum draws particular attention to the fact that governance in the MDC—which is based on key mechanisms, such as political champions, a networked institutional structure, the fast-tracking of design and implementation and so on—is designed for the facilitation and implementation of "bankable" private investment projects and public-private partnerships (PPPs). However, such a framework contains serious limitations with regard to participation, democracy, and the integration of provincial and local governments and communities in the process. This experience is important to recognise in governing other future SDIs and development corridors in southern Africa.

Xenia Ngwenya and Ian Taylor focus, in chapter 6, on PPPs. The chapter begins with the role of the Economic Commission for Africa (ECA) in pushing market-based solutions to Africa's development impasse and how the PPP model is concomitantly advanced in the MDC. The chapter in particular looks at how PPPs in the transport sector have impacted upon local communities in the MDC area. The N4 toll road from Witbank to Maputo is a case in point. The authors situate the need of the MDC for a reconstructed infrastructural network within its historical context, briefly touching on the part played by the apartheid state in sabotaging much of the previously existent transport networks. The role of private and commercial agents in renewing the various infrastructure projects is analysed, as is the political controversy that has followed much of the processes. The lessons that can be learnt from the MDC are teased out, in light of the fact that the PPP approach is gaining momentum in Africa.

James Hentz's chapter starts out looking at the negotiations leading to the creation of the Mozal aluminium smelter, including the role played by the two governments (Mozambique and South Africa) as well as foreign institutions and investors. Mozal is the largest single investment project in Mozambique worth US$1.3 billion, which almost equals the GDP of the country. The project has been actively promoted by not only the Mozambican but also the South African government and foreign institutions. Hentz investigates why and how this mega-project became a reality, its underlying economic rationale and, importantly, its impact on the Mozambican economy. The broader development effects (such as job creation, human resource development, gender, ecology and social development) and local responses and protests to the project are detailed, with some lessons to be learnt for future SDIs.

In chapter 8, Irâe Baptista-Lundin and Ian Taylor provide a "view from Maputo". By way of historically situating Mozambique's reform process under Frelimo and the resultant "policy fit" between Frelimo and the ANC, governance and development issues in Mozambique are analysed, as are emerging resistances from "below". In concentrating on activities on the ground, the authors also outline the vibrant cross-border flows of Mozambican labour migrants and informal traders who for centuries have created the dense social fabric of the "real" Maputo Corridor.

Finally, Fredrik Söderbaum and Ian Taylor wrap the volume up with overall empirical and theoretical conclusions that can be drawn from the study, concentrating on the two key focus areas of the volume: governance and development. In this regard, the conclusion asks again who is included/excluded, and who benefits and who does not from the MDC. The chapter also seeks to draw policy lessons from the MDC and outlines some implications for future SDIs in southern Africa.

Chapter 2

The Maputo Development Corridor: Progress Achieved and Lessons Learned

Geoff de Beer and David Arkwright

The Maputo Development Corridor Spatial Development Initiative was the first of the SDIs to be implemented in 1995. The Maputo Development Corridor (MDC) is essentially an economic corridor linking Gauteng province in South Africa, (the economic heartland of the South African economy) to its closest port, namely Maputo in Mozambique. The MDC initiative focuses on the rehabilitation and upgrading of trade and transport links as a basis for encouraging a broad economic development of the area. In this chapter we review the MDC experience in terms of a number of key aspects. The analysis starts with an overview of, first, the MDC's main objectives and strategies. Secondly, we look at its underlying design principles. After this, an overview is provided of the main infrastructure and economic development projects and technical support programmes. Following on from this is a brief assessment of progress achieved thus far, highlighting a number of the key lessons that have been gleaned from the MDC process. Finally, we highlight some of the key strengths and weaknesses of the MDC experience.

Key Objectives and Strategies

The MDC was initiated on the basis of four objectives. They were firstly, to rehabilitate the core infrastructure along the MDC with minimum impact on the fiscus. Secondly, to maximise investment in both the inherent potential of the MDC area and in the added opportunities which infrastructure rehabilitation creates. Thirdly, to ensure that the development impact of this investment is maximised, particularly with regard to disadvantaged communities. Fourthly, to ensure sustainability by developing policy, strategies and frameworks that encompasses a holistic, participatory and integrated approach to development.

The initial key strategies targeted the rehabilitation of the core transport infrastructure through public-private partnerships (PPPs) (see Ngwenya and Taylor, chapter 6). Focus areas for infrastructure rehabilitation were the upgrading/construction of a toll road linking Johannesburg in South Africa to

Maputo in Mozambique and the improvement of rail and port operations in Mozambique to re-establish competitiveness of the transport route. The planning process adopted reflected the trans-national character of the initiative, and was characterised by deliberate "quick step" planning and decision-making processes (see Söderbaum, chapter 5). In order to support the initiative and to manage key policy shifts, the political leadership in each country undertook to put in place inter-sectoral co-ordinating bodies at the ministerial and technical levels, intended to facilitate work within each country as well as to co-ordinate activities bi-nationally. The political leaders also took steps to publicly champion and drive forward the initiative. Further, it was decided to create a bi-national promotional entity, the Maputo Corridor Company (MCC), which although not constituted legally, was intended to be an important promotional and facilitating entity.

In addition to the above objectives and strategies, it is evident that since 1997 there were certain shifts in emphasis and priority between objectives and strategies. These changes in emphasis were in response to varying levels of progress being achieved with the initial objectives set. Firstly, as progress was made with implementation of the core infrastructure and economic development projects (also referred to as the "mega-projects"), greater emphasis was placed on the third of the original objectives of the MDC (to ensure that the development impact of this investment is maximised, particularly to disadvantaged communities). Underlying this shift in priority was an acceptance that these "mega-projects" were unlikely to produce large numbers of low cost jobs, or spontaneously (i.e. "trickle-down") to promote large numbers of sustainable entrepreneurial development opportunities (see Söderbaum and Taylor, chapter 4). Neither were such projects likely to provide opportunities for community based empowerment projects. Within this context, greater emphasis was placed on the identification of potential pilot demonstration projects in the agriculture, forestry, and tourism sectors; small, micro and medium scale enterprise (SMME) development programmes; and local economic development (LED).

As part of the original MDC objective and in support of a greater priority being placed on tourism, forestry and agriculture, a related policy research programme was launched in early 1998. The main focus of this research programme was directly influenced by issues requiring attention in terms of the better utilisation of the corridor's inherent development potential in terms of forestry, tourism and agriculture. Focus areas included: local and international best practice for community based, and community/public/private partnership based forestry development; regional approaches to the marketing, management and development of tourism; and international perspectives on transboundary development in the case of asymmetric economies. This became the basis for the Borderlands Programme, aimed at facilitating conscious transboundary collaboration processes that recognised the dynamics of the region and which brought to bear international best practices in transboundary systems and programmes. Key initiatives in this regard were the establishment of a co-operative, multinational research and capacity building mechanism, the restructuring of the micro-region's border posts, an assessment of the micro-region's environmental management framework, and the building of transboundary institutional structures and systems.

To ensure sustainability by developing strategies and frameworks that encompassed a holistic, participatory and integrated approach to development, a capacity building programme was also launched in early 1998. This programme was targeted at building the capacity of the Mpumalanga provincial (and where possible the Mozambican) government officials involved in the MDC.

Key Principles Underpinning the MDC Initiative

There were a number of key principles that underpinned the MDC initiative. Prime among these was co-operation, collaboration and integration in terms of economic policy and strategy. Prior to the political changes in South Africa, the rest of the region had not been able to design and implement collaborative and integrated economic policies and strategies that included South Africa. With a democratic government coming into power in South Africa, political obstacles were removed, and immediately there was an increased emphasis on economic collaboration and integration. The key economic benefits that were to be derived by South Africa and Mozambique (and to a lesser extent Swaziland) from this new regionally co-operative and integrated approach were seen to include those benefits typically associated with regional integration. These might be briefly summarised as enhanced scale economies; the promotion of competition and innovation at a regional level; the provision of a stimulus to investment and productivity; the institutionalisation of conflict management; reduced economic disparities and inequities among southern African countries; and enhanced bargaining in international fora (Jourdan et al., 1996; Arkwright et al., 1998).

A focus on existing transportation/development corridors was also a key principle of the MDC. There are two main aspects to note in this regard. Firstly, the MDC was not a new creation: the transportation corridor between Gauteng and Maputo developed over decades in response to the prevailing space economy (see Söderbaum and Taylor, chapter 1). Its functioning was halted directly as a result of definable political conflicts between the previous South African government and Mozambique. The MDC in this sense represents a "simple" focus on rehabilitating, upgrading and in certain instances supplementing the main strategic infrastructure linking Gauteng and Maputo, and allowing the economy to operate more normally. Secondly, the MDC was selected as a priority for public sector support (financial, technical and political) specifically because of its inherent, but under-utilised, potential for sustainable economic development.

From the outset it was stressed that the SDI methodology/concept could not simply be applied anywhere (Jourdan et al., 1996). Indeed, the long-term sustainability and success of the MDC was to be based on the existence of its proven, inherent, under-utilised economic development potential. Connected to this was the promotion of development corridors rather than transportation routes. The MDC approach placed emphasis on developing this transportation corridor not only as a transportation route linking a resource rich area with its closest coastal ports, or even linking a few nodes along a transportation route, but rather on simultaneously exploiting the variety of other development opportunities that arise along the route. Thus the emphasis was placed on identifying and exploiting the supplementary economic investment and development opportunities arising by virtue of locational advantages in relation to enhanced transportation networks. This in itself would stimulate greater regional competitiveness via regional integration and collaboration. Indeed, the main opportunities to be achieved via this new approach were seen to include the diversification of the region's industrial base based on both Mozambique and South Africa's inherent development potential and related comparative advantages. The two countries' industrial specialisation and a regional approach to the mobilisation of FDI and the sharing of the micro-region's training and capacity building skills would also be enlisted.

A more controversial principle underpinning the MDC was the great emphasis on the role of the private sector. This "crowding in" of the private sector typically took two predominant forms. Firstly, whereas the private sector had in the past not been allowed to develop and operate certain elements of public infrastructure (such as regional roads and railways) the South African and Mozambique governments changed policy to actively encourage, support and facilitate the involvement of the private sector in such areas (Ngwenya and Taylor, chapter 6). A second aspect of this "crowding in" approach was something of a by-product, but one that was vitally important nevertheless. By crowding in a greater number of individual private sector investors, developers and operators into a particular geographical area there appeared to be a perceived and real lessening of investment risk for the private sector, whilst at the same time providing positive marketing and development momentum for the investment area.

Progress with the Major Projects and Support Programmes

The major elements of the MDC can be broadly categorised into: the major infrastructure projects; the major economic development projects; and the technical and institutional support programmes.

The Major Infrastructure Projects

With regard to the major infrastructure projects, a number of key developments may be identified. Prime among these is the reconstruction and development of the Witbank-Maputo N4 toll road (Ngwenya and Taylor, chapter 6). Trans African Concessions (TRAC) was awarded a thirty-year concession in 1997 and reconstruction of the road has been completed at a cost of US$250 million. This project has elicited significant concern from communities down its length, including issues of constitutionality, toll fees, affordability and impact on the local economy. The learning curve has been steep for all concerned. The project's contribution to SMME development (702 contracts in construction to a value of US$38 million), to job creation (6,220 permanent, temporary and casual), and to training (20,260 people through various training programmes to date) has, it must be said, already been significant. The medium to long-term benefits of this project include guarantees on the road quality, safety and travelling times over the concession period, and the substantial business employment generation still to be obtained from further road construction and long term maintenance. Opportunities that will arise from the constantly improving logistics should also be mentioned in this regard.

Perhaps second in prominence within the MDC is the rehabilitation of the port of Maputo. The Mozambique government has reached an "in principle" agreement for a fifteen year management contract with Merseyside Docks and Harbour Company (MDHC) to finance and undertake the rehabilitation of the port, at a cost of some US$65 million, and also to manage it. MDHC has placed a suspensive condition in the draft agreement to the effect that the rail concession must be satisfactorily concluded before they will sign the management agreement. In anticipation of the suspensive condition being met, MDHC has proceeded with much of the technical work associated with the planned upgrade. Thus the Mozambique government has decided to concession the southern Mozambique rail network in two parts. Agreement has been reached on the concessioning of the first part, namely the Limpopo line to Zimbabwe, the Goba line to Swaziland and the marshalling yards at Maputo. The second part is the Ressano Garcia line to South Africa, and in this regard Spoornet (the South African rail parastatal) has been identified as the preferred bidder. So far however, the parties have been unable to reach agreement on the terms of the concession.

Worthy of note is the development of two new 400 kilovolt electricity lines from South Africa into southern Mozambique. Eskom (South Africa), EDM (Mozambique) and the Swaziland Electricity Board have joined forces in the implementation of this project known as Motraco. The lines have been built and the project is now supplying electricity to the Mozambique Aluminium Smelter (Mozal). It is a long-term objective of this project to supply electricity to urban and rural areas in Swaziland and in southern Mozambique.

Finally, the upgrading of the Ressano Garcia border post between South Africa and Mozambique is another major project of the MDC. In a test case for new approaches to border posts within southern Africa, there has been a move away from the traditional border post model to a concept that simultaneously deals with managing illegal movement whilst speedily facilitating legal movement. The first phase of such an approach is now underway at a cost of US$ five million and includes the development of a pre-clearance facility for commercial traffic away from the border post and certain improvements to the facilities at the border post itself to facilitate movement.

The Major Economic Development Projects

Having discussed the major infrastructure projects within the MDC, the major economic projects need to be analysed. Prime among these is the development of the Mozal (Hentz, chapter 7). This is a world-class, low cost and high quality aluminium smelter, situated just outside the city of Maputo. Established initially to produce 250,000 tons of aluminium per year, a decision was subsequently taken to double the capacity of the smelter, bringing the construction value up to US$ two billion and future output to 500,000 tons of aluminium per year. The feed stocks for the smelter come in from Australia and the bulk of the aluminium is to be exported to Japan. A dedicated port terminal has been constructed at Matola for this purpose. A linkage programme has been initiated to look at upstream, sidestream and downstream opportunities around this substantial project. Already some two hundred projects with a value of US$100 million have been identified for Mozambican companies and for joint venture operations involving companies from outside Mozambique, including South Africa. Mozal has, and will continue to have, a powerful impact on the Mozambique economy and that of the region. Its potential in generating an industrial base in southern Mozambique is very significant.

Adjacent to Mozal, the government of Mozambique has encouraged the establishment of an industrial free zone, known as the Beluluane Industrial Park (BIP). This is a joint venture, involving the Investment Promotion Centre of Mozambique (CPI), Chiefton (Australia) and Grinaker (South Africa). Comprising some 600 hectares, the BIP aims to attract a mix of foreign, regional and local investment into heavy industry, manufacturing and hi-tech industries. The key features of BIP are industrial free zone status (with a variety of attractive fiscal and other incentives), state of the art infrastructure, good access, a linkage programme into the local economy and turn-key development capacity. Whilst a range of industries has already expressed interest in locating within BIP, progress has however been slow. Three small companies servicing Mozal are busy locating to BIP and the World Bank is currently appraising a possible loan to the project for a further phase of infrastructure development. The reasons for the slow progress include the cautious approach by the developers, no clear industrial strategy and the lack of progress in resolving transboundary issues between South Africa and Mozambique—including perceptions of the high costs in Mozambique.

Following successful exploration in the Temane gas field in Mozambique and a more recent acquisition of exploration rights in the Pande gas field in Mozambique, Sasol is now involved in the exploitation of natural gas within the MDC. Sasol plans to construct a US$ one billion, 1,000 km pipeline from the gas fields of Mozambique to Secunda in Mpumalanga. The initial customers for such a pipeline are considered to be the Maputo Iron and Steel Project, Sasol itself (in Sasolburg and Secunda as key feedstock for fuel and chemical plants) and potentially some 600 industries that are already linked to a Sasol gas supply line inside South Africa. In the longer term, gas could also provide impetus to a petrochemical industry in Mozambique, with indicators already that Sasol has acquired the technology for diesel fuel production from gas.

Besides the above-mentioned "mega-projects", there has been considerable investment to meet the demands in the mining sector (new and expansion projects in nickel, chrome and coal in Mpumalanga); in agriculture (specifically the rapid growth in the sugar industry); in tourism (with new tourism being developed in Mpumalanga, Mozambique and Swaziland); in commerce (with substantial new commercial outlets in Maputo and Nelspruit); in transport; and in the development of health and educational facilities. In short, it is estimated that some US$600 million in mainly private sector investment has been committed to the key infrastructure projects, and a further US$5,500 million to the key sector investments. It has been conservatively calculated that this investment has created some 15,000 permanent jobs. People movement between Mozambique and South Africa through the border post has shown an increase of 27 per cent per annum over the past six years, whilst imports and exports through the border post have shown increases of 58 per cent and 55 per cent per annum respectively over the past five years.

The Technical and Institutional Support Programme

Specific technical support programmes have been implemented to support the MDC. Amongst the most important have been the cluster and linkage processes, policy research and capacity building, and strategic environmental management (see Söderbaum and Taylor, chapter 4). Other support programmes undertaken, but not discussed here, include local economic development in twenty-six small towns, the development of pilot projects in various sectors, a communications strategy for the MDC and various sectoral strategies.

The cluster studies and linkage programmes were initiated in 1997. In Mpumalanga these initiatives focus on the timber industry in Piet Retief, the steel and stainless steel industry in Middleburg/Witbank, tourism-led development in the Trout Triangle (Belfast, Machadadorp, Dullstroom), wool industries in Ermelo, the furniture industry in White River, agro-processing in Nkomazi and the petrochemical industries in Secunda. In Mozambique, the focus to date has been on the aluminium industry related to Mozal. Progress with the process in Mpumalanga remains slow and the main constraint has been the lack of funding from both the provincial and national government levels.

In 1998, the policy research and capacity building programme was initiated with the support of Britain's Department for International Development (DFID), to assess and learn from international best practice in key areas such as tourism-led development, models for community empowerment, and best practice for border control. However, whilst delivering a number of key inputs in its first year of operation, the policy research programme was severely disrupted by the sudden withdrawal of DFID finance at the end of the first of an anticipated three-year-period. Indeed, whilst up and running the capacity building programme provided training to thirty-eight project managers from Mpumalanga and six from Mozambique, but once the DFID funding was removed, further implementation of the programme was largely stopped.

Nevertheless, during the year of its operation, the policy research programmes were able to complete best practice assessments in terms of regional approaches to tourism marketing, management and development. This research was intended to support the activities of the South East Africa Tourism Committee (SEATOC), which is still operational and is playing an increasingly prominent role in the marketing, management and development of tourism in the Mpumalanga, Swaziland, southern Mozambique and northern KwaZulu.

It should be noted that the best practice analysis of trans-frontier collaboration by economically asymmetric economies was completed as well. The primary area of analysis was the US/Mexico border (seen as an example of classic asymmetric economies) as well as drawing on other similar experiences in Europe. This analysis was followed up by a visit by a joint Mozambique/South Africa team to Mexico and California and a subsequent reciprocal visit by San Diego State University and city representatives of San Diego to observe processes in the South African borderland areas. This led to a decision by Mpumalanga, Swaziland and Mozambique to establish a transboundary Borderlands Committee, noted above. However, this initiative also fell foul of the funding crises and was also impacted on by political shifts in Mpumalanga.

One of the more significant trans-frontier collaboration projects to survive the above, has been the Swaziland/South Africa Tourism and Biodiversity Corridor Initiative (a transboundary tourism and conservation based development initiative), which has now been successfully launched with considerable private sector investment and public sector support to infrastructure development. On the Swaziland side, funding has been secured to facilitate the planning and development process. This initiative has been characterised by very high levels of local level "buy-in", including the Barberton Chamber of Commerce, the Borderlands Regional Tourism Organisation (South Africa and Swaziland), local community organisations, local political parties, and private sector landowners and businesses. This has had a positive impact in terms of decision-making and dispute resolution, and has also provided a far greater focus on local economic development issues, as well as the need for private sector participation etc.

Regarding strategic management, a Strategic Environmental Management Plan (SEMP) was drawn up for the South African of the MDC in 1997/98, and subsequently, through the Borderlands Committee, an initiative was started for Swaziland and southern Mozambique. However, again due to funding problems and capacity issues, the initiative did not get off the ground and the SEMP has never been properly implemented.

Of note was the development of appropriate institutional structures to manage the MDC (see Söderbaum, chapter 5). In 1995 the South African Department of Transport established a technical team drawn from the Development Bank of Southern Africa (DBSA), the Industrial Development Corporation of South Africa (IDC) and the Council for Scientific and Industrial Research (CSIR) to provide technical support to an inter-departmental committee at national government level. Mozambique developed a similar inter-departmental working committee, but drew on consultants for the technical work and interface from South Africa. In 1996 the South African Department of Transport assisted in establishing a technical unit in Mpumalanga, providing funding for a technical support programme at the provincial level. Mozambique did not pursue a similar process.

In 1997 South Africa and Mozambique agreed to establish the Maputo Corridor Company (MCC) as a facilitating entity, comprising public and private sectors of South Africa, Mozambique and immediate SADC neighbours. The MCC has remained a public sector supported facilitating entity. In Mozambique, the recent formation of co-ordinating structures in government will compliment those already existing in South Africa and Swaziland. Mozambique has created a permanent capacity as well as a national support capacity in the Transport and Communications Ministry. A process of dialogue has also opened up between the investment and marketing agencies in the broader southern African region. The South African government has also established a regional SDI co-ordinator post, and the South African Department of Trade and Industry (DTI) has made budgetary provision for supporting selected regional SDIs. This suggests a long-term commitment to these processes by the South African government.

Lessons of Experience Arising

A number of important lessons of experience can be derived from the MDC experience thus far. Firstly, socio-political stability is a vital condition for broad-based investor mobilisation. The situation where one tries to promote SDIs in the context of real and/or perceived political unrest (such as currently in Zimbabwe) is very difficult and unlikely to succeed. Similarly, all investors require a reasonable degree of macro-economic stability and a sound regulatory framework. In addition, for a SDI to prosper, it has to be selected on the basis of very strong inherent and under-utilised development potential. The MDC was a historically proven transportation corridor. In this regard the rehabilitation, upgrading and supplementing of the transport infrastructure in this corridor, and the conversion of this corridor from a transport to development corridor was all but assured since the inherent development potential was easy to establish.

Connected to this, the upfront identification of anchor and lead investment projects is vital for generating development momentum. Critical to the success of the MDC was the ability to identify and implement a set of strategic anchor projects. Experience with this SDI, as well as similar development interventions internationally, is that it is easier to get countries to agree on a few specific collaboration projects than it is to agree on comprehensive transboundary development programmes. The same experience indicates that once investors have been mobilised on the anchor projects, this achievement contributes much to the initiative in terms of demonstrating that the "hype is real".

Success is thus dependent on identifying an integrated set of economic and infrastructure projects rather than single and/or disjointed projects. In order to successfully mobilise private sector investors, it is essential to demonstrate that the intended investment projects are financially viable. Related to this, private sector financiers and investors needed to see and understand three key inter-relationships. Firstly, the inter-relationships between the various elements of infrastructure. Secondly, the inter-relationships between the economic development projects. Thirdly, the inter-relationships between the infrastructure and economic development projects.

In order to be able to identify and package the set of economically and financially viable investment projects, it was essential for the South Africa and Mozambique governments to mobilise a strong technical capacity to support the project identification, conceptualisation and packaging processes. A related issue that arose in the course of the MDC initiative was the need to ensure that the bidding and adjudication processes were perceived to be transparent and fair. This is crucial in order to attract high profile, world class investors, who are vital in generating further investment. Part of getting anchor projects established was the identification and securing of high profile, good quality investors. The significance of such investors was well demonstrated with Mozal, and similar trends have been observed internationally in Subic Bay in the Philippines (with FedEx) and in Cancun in Mexico (with leading international hotel chains). In all these instances successful investments by the lead investors had the spin-off effect of attracting considerable smaller investors, many of whom either have upstream or downstream linkages to the lead investments, or are potential competitors, and thus contribute to the "clustering" effect.

The experience of the MDC has also highlighted the fact that projects need to be marketed to investors in different ways. With particular regard to tourism, the approach that was typically applied in the early stages of the MDC was one where the South African government, having decided that it would allow private sector investment into a certain locality and having undertaken the necessary "packaging", then placed adverts in the local media and internet and requested proposals from the private sector. This approach had worked very well in the context of the N4 toll road, and it also produced reasonable results in terms of getting interest from local South African investors. It did not however attract any real interest from international tourism investors or operators. Interactions with leading international tourism organisations and with tourism investor mobilisation consultancies confirmed that the leading international investors are currently being offered, or are considering, many large investment opportunities at any one time. They do not generally peruse the media for new investment opportunities. Rather, opportunities are brought to them, or are routed through advisors who are aware of the investor requirements, conditions and so on.

On a cautionary note, it needs to be acknowledged that the application of the SDI methodology is not something that should, or was ever intended to, replace normal national or provincial development planning processes. The SDI methodology was deliberately very focused geographically and economically and was geared to identifying and securing initial high profile strategic investment opportunities. Once these anchor projects had been identified and investors secured, it was important that these initial SDI efforts were supplemented by a more broadly based socio-economic development planning process. This latter type of intervention (not especially well applied in the case of the MDC) is vital to the long-term success of a SDI. This is particularly so in terms of identifying a broader range of investment opportunities that arise from improved infrastructure, as spin-offs from the lead projects and as a result of greater investor awareness and confidence. These upstream, downstream, competitive and service industries are likely to be important in achieving more cost effective employment creation and in stimulating local investment opportunities.

Furthermore, the type of intervention made as part of the MDC project was quite specific. When the MDC was initiated, one of the key objectives was to implement the planning and decision making process at great speed (see

Söderbaum, chapter 5). This was primarily in order to boost development momentum. This high-speed character was also intended to distinguish the development process from normal day-to-day development planning processes in the public sector. In reality it has been found that the original one year time framework from commencement to investor mobilisation around selected "anchor projects" was too optimistic. Even though the MDC process was implemented within this time frame in terms of the initial investment projects, practice has shown that the initiative needed to be pursued with national government support for far longer than this. This is primarily because the lower levels of government have battled to develop their own capacity to run with the programme.

Another lesson learnt was that in order to be able to implement the SDI approach in a regional (i.e. multi-country) context, it was essential that there was direct support and involvement at the top political level (see Söderbaum, chapter 5). The MDC, with the Ministers of Transport from Mozambique and South Africa was a very good example of this. This ties in with the fact that in the context of a critical capital and technical resource shortages in southern Africa, the successful implementation of the MDC was reliant on the participation of a strong and willing local and regional and international private sector. This is unlikely if there is not strong state support (see Söderbaum and Taylor, chapter 4).

Thus there is a need for technical, political, economic, institutional and legally sound strategies and projects. Such aspects need to be addressed at both the project as well as policy and strategy level. These skills were generally in short supply during the launch of the MDC, and often additional expertise was needed to be imported into southern African countries. Considerable care needed to be taken in ensuring that opportunities to develop local more permanent skills were attended to and for this reason it was important that capacity building programmes were designed to build required skills. In certain instances this capacity building took the form of stand alone training programmes, but in many instances there was considerable learning and capacity building opportunities achieved by involving local expertise alongside hired outside expertise.

Conclusion

Rather than only creating an enabling environment, the SDI approach as applied in the case of the MDC was intended to promote a direct, high profile, well resourced, spatially focused, economically and financially sound project-oriented intervention as a key strategy in promoting regional integration and enhancing trade. In the case of the MDC the focus was clearly related to the reconstruction and simultaneous conversion of an historic transportation corridor and trade route to a multi-sectoral development corridor. Critical to the implementation of the MDC was the adherence to areas of inherent development potential, a focus on projects and programmes that were economically and financially viable, and a far greater role for the private sector due to their key strengths related to capital and expertise.

Measured against the strategic objectives agreed to for the MDC, this initiative has been relatively successful in terms of implementing key initial infrastructure and economic investment projects. It has also achieved in terms of the mobilisation of private sector investment and the creation of sustainable employment opportunities, albeit the initial employment opportunities were very capital intensive in nature.

The key principles underpinning the SDI approach now appear to be increasingly well accepted in the southern African context. It is too early to gauge the long-term impacts on socio-economic development, though indications from the MDC demonstrate some positive developmental impacts. Notwithstanding the success stories, there are potential areas of weakness (see Söderbaum and Taylor, chapter 4; Söderbaum, chapter 5; Ngwenya and Taylor, chapter 6; Hentz, chapter 7). The most serious of these are associated with the attempt to spontaneously create upstream and downstream linkages and the inability to generate large numbers of low-cost employment opportunities. It is clear that the level of progress in terms of the identification, preparation and implementation of pilot projects was severely impacted upon by the financial and technical capacity constraints experienced by the Mpumalanga government. This situation was made worse by the political changes that took place in the province at the end of 1999, which had the effect of reducing available technical support capacity from the provincial government for the initiative. It also created considerable uncertainty about the nature and extent of Mpumalanga's support for the MDC as a whole.

In addition, the decision by DFID to withdraw its funding after the first of a planned three year development programme, combined with the inability to secure alternative additional funds by those managing the MDC process, had a huge impact on the programme. Certainly, it resulted in many elements of the programme being halted or cut short. Typically, this has meant that those programmes focused on tourism-led, agriculture-led and forestry-led development have been worse affected. This in turn has impacted on local economic development initiatives.

There are a number of observations that can be made regarding the development planning and decision-making approaches that have characterised the MDC. From the outset of the launch of the idea of SDIs the relative pros and cons of centralised and high speed planning and decision making processes were discussed (Jourdan et al., 1996). Even at this early stage it was highlighted that the SDI approach would be effective in terms of getting projects on the ground as quickly as possible, but that this approach could easily result in a situation where individuals and lower levels of government felt excluded. Whilst there has been tremendous progress with implementing the various anchor projects, these negatives have clearly emerged in practice. The lesson that can be learnt for future initiatives such as this is that it is imperative that national and provincial government (particularly at the most senior political levels, but also at a senior official level) maintain a very regular dialogue and keep each other properly informed.

In context of the above point, as well as the strategic objective of developing a highly diverse and integrated economic development corridor between Gauteng and Maputo, one must assume that particularly the Mpumalanga and Maputo provinces had a major responsibility for the MDC planning and development processes. The national interventions were international and were strategically vital, but they needed to be accepted as supplementary to ongoing provincial activities. However, looking back on the development process over the past six years it seems that the practice has been somewhat different. The combination of a very centralised and dominant approach from national government (in the case of South Africa anyway), combined with important changes at a political and official level in Mpumalanga since the end of 1999, have resulted in a situation where Mpumalanga has not been able to effectively take on the broader development planning and project programming processes. Looking ahead there is at present no evidence to suggest that Mpumalanga has a plan or strategy in place to take over the MDC initiative. This too will impact on the development momentum in the future.

Yet, the SDI type approach as was originally applied in the MDC was one intended to be fundamentally based in economic reality, and one that was sensitive to the requirements of the investor community. The approach was not one that "waits for the market to operate" as a means of generating economic growth and development. If anything, the approach was one that presupposed a tendency for market failure, or at least a very slowly responding market. As such, the SDI approach is one that is extremely pro-active and in order to succeed vitally needs a supportive environment at the policy level, through plans and strategies.

Notwithstanding some of the positive points mentioned above, it appears that the MDC initiative (in the South African context and probably in the Mozambique context) has become increasingly characterised by some of the "bottlenecks" that the SDI methodology aimed to avoid. Despite concerns being raised by the private sector to government to take the MDC initiative more seriously, the initiative has become characterised by a lack of political leadership (either nationally or provincially in South Africa). This has meant a very slow decision making process, resulting in very few—if any—new practical project interventions and a general lack of support from government bureaucracy. A shortage of funds to implement studies, projects and programmes makes the situation worse. Unless the MDC initiative receives some urgent political support and a priority commitment to raise its profile and performance, there appears to be a very good chance that the MDC that became the success story that launched other regional SDIs will slowly fade into oblivion. Furthermore, the SDI methodology, which could conceivably play an important role in the New Partnership for Africa's Development (NEPAD), will also probably become discredited.

Chapter 3

Situating the Maputo Corridor: A Regional Perspective

Daniel Tevera and Admos Chimhowu

Dominant analyses of regional economic integration suggest that it provides a stimulus for economic growth through the increased commercial opportunities made available. It is argued that regional co-operation in sectors such as transport and communications enable landlocked countries to have access to port facilities, thereby increasing their capacities to trade internationally. According to Oyejide (1998) regional integration empowers countries to produce goods at lower unit costs for a larger regional market. Economic regionalism is therefore partly necessitated by the varying size of the national economies. This is particularly true for southern Africa where the existence of small economies has arguably hindered the emergence and development of national enterprises that can compete internationally. However, regional economic integration requires appropriate spatial dimensional variates that can effectively reintegrate inter-state markets. The strategy to deal with this thus far has been to deal with macro-territorial integration issues through the formation of organisations, such as the Southern African Development Community (SADC), whose main emphasis has been to promote inter-state co-operation through the harmonisation of development strategies and the utilization of shared natural resources, including watersheds. A more recent approach has been through the establishment of spatial development initiatives (SDIs), which have been at the very core of strategies to promote regional co-operation in southern Africa since the late 1990s.

Ever since, a number of regional integration initiatives in southern Africa have been driven by cross border investments, primarily by South African quasi-state bodies and related private capital initiatives. Following the demise of apartheid in 1994 the South African government, first led by former President Nelson Mandela and now by President Thabo Mbeki, has introduced neo-liberal trade, investment and fiscal policies with considerable spatial manifestations. The most concerted effort with a potential to have significant impact on both the South African and regional space economies have been the SDI programmes, which were first launched in 1995 (see Söderbaum and Taylor, chapter 1).

The SDI programme is essentially aimed at stimulating economic growth by creating globally competitive spatial entities through new investment, infrastructural development and job creation. Basically, SDIs are export-oriented industrial development strategies that have led to a rebirth of "corridors". Following years of apartheid, economic sanctions and an industrial policy geared towards import substitution, the new SDI programme has become a crucial vehicle for reorienting the South African economy and for generating regional development. By linking industries with a well-developed transport route network, the development corridors are expected to encourage the development of both forward and backward linkages (Harrison and Todes, 2001). All these initiatives are meant to take advantage of the inherent development potential of existing nascent regions. Since several of the development corridors span national boundaries (for instance, the MDC), they have the potential to strengthen the linkages between neighbouring countries. However, Nel (2002) sounds a cautionary note with his observation that despite the considerable support given to the South African SDIs most of them have not been able to bring about economic transformation in the areas that they straddle. Most of the SDIs are located on the coast, reflecting the export orientation of the post-apartheid economic development policies and government's need to redirect economic growth from the resource rich Gauteng province, which historically has been the economic core of the country. It also reflects the perceived geographic advantage that coastal spaces hold as a conduit for exports to the global economy.

The aims of this chapter are twofold. Firstly, it seeks to examine the corridor concept as a framework for regional development in southern Africa and uses the MDC as a case study. Secondly, it explores the extent to which the goals of the MDC resonate with SADC's aim to promote regional economic development through regional co-operation and integration. The analysis starts out, in the next section, with the observation that corridors are not a new phenomena and that there are other types of spatial and regional frameworks for development in southern Africa. The second section discusses the emergence of the MDC, whereas the third concentrates on some of the (uneven) developmental impacts of the MDC. Before briefly rounding up the analysis, the fourth section discusses the relationship between the MDC and SADC.

Corridors and Other Regional Frameworks for Development

Corridors are by no means a new phenomenon in southern Africa, primarily mainly in the form of transport routes. Ironically, these were developed either during the colonial period as transport corridors, or during the days of apartheid as a means to reduce the neighbouring front-line states' dependence on South Africa and provide a shorter access to the sea for land-locked Zimbabwe, Zambia and Botswana. A good example of transport corridors as a means to circumvent South Africa is the Beira corridor, whose rail and road network links the Zimbabwean border city of Mutare with the Mozambican port of Beira. The predecessor of SADC, the

Southern African Development Co-ordination Conference (SADCC), was able to mobilise a substantial amount of donor funding during the 1980s in order to develop the Beira corridor. Little attempt was however made to link this and other transport corridors, such as Nacala and Maputo, to the development of the local space economies that they traversed. Not surprisingly, no local industrial or commercial agricultural projects emerged along these corridors in Mozambique.

The near absence of any policy pronouncements on spatial frameworks in southern Africa implies that whatever possibilities for micro-regionalism that existed in the past were adversely affected by the absence of support institutions. Currently, SADC does not have a deliberate policy to mainstream spatial frameworks at the supranational level, yet this is one of the prerequisites for the development of micro-regionalism involving several countries. As will be further discussed later in this chapter, the absence of an operational and adequately funded supranational or regional spatial planning unit makes the future of micro-regionalism at the SADC level problematic. Certainly, in the absence of SADC-level spatial frameworks, development corridors will remain an initiative confined to South Africa, Mozambique, Namibia, Botswana and Zimbabwe.

South Africa's SDI programme is undoubtedly the most advanced and distinct of all existing micro-regional frameworks in southern Africa. Five types of development corridors are in operation in South Africa. These are: (i) industrial SDIs, such as the one stretching from Richards Bay to Durban/Pietermaritzburg; (ii) agri-tourism SDIs, such as the Wild Coast and the Lubombo Development Corridor; (iii) focused industrial development areas, including the Industrial Development Zones around airports and seaports; (iv) mixed industrial and agri-tourism, such as the Maputo Development Corridor; and (v) metropolitan corridors, exemplified by the Cape Town Corridor from Phillipi to Wynberg. There are at least ten sites in South Africa where SDIs have been established and several of these overlap with national parks and nature reserves.

Corridors and SDIs are however by no means the only frameworks for regional development in southern Africa. High profile examples of other types of cross border investments driven first and foremost by South African capital also exist. The Lesotho Highlands Water Project, which provides the South African industrial heartland of Gauteng with water is a classic example. Eskom, the electricity utility company, has invested extensively in the expansion of the Cahora Bassa Dam in Mozambique, whilst South African white farmers have been given long term leases to prime agricultural land in both Mozambique and Zambia. In addition, Sasol has a major stake in the construction of the 895km natural gas pipeline (costing R4.8 million) from gas fields in Mozambique's Inhambane province to the massive petrochemical complex at Secunda in South Africa's Mpumalanga province whilst tourism investments by South African and Mozambican elites in the Vilanculos Coastal Wildlife Sanctuary in Mozambique (MacLeod, 2001); and the establishment of the 35,000 square km Gaza-Kruger-Gonarezhou Trans-frontier Park (GKG), bringing together South Africa, Zimbabwe and Mozambique, represents an intriguing example of environmental co-operation (GKG, 2000).

These new cross border investment initiatives, driven first and foremost by South African companies have generated considerable debate. The governments of Mozambique, Zambia and South Africa are of the opinion that the initiatives provide good examples whereby the state and private sector can work closely on development projects. In the same vein, SADC sees these initiatives as "strategic alliances". In fact, when acting as the SADC chairman at one of the regional summits in November 2000, President Chissano of Mozambique argued that just as the national governments are engaged in dynamic co-operation, the private sector in different countries should establish "partnerships" and business links that promote regional development (see Söderbaum and Taylor, chapter 4; Ngwenya and Taylor, chapter 6; Hentz, chapter 7). However, critical scholars view the "strategic alliances" as post-colonial discursive constructions that are based on the use of private capital in order to establish zones of influence, without incurring direct costs. Mudenda (2000) has shown that there is a growing resentment of South African investments within the SADC region in sectors such as tourism, transport corridors, sea ports, agriculture and mining. The fear that South Africa is somehow "colonising" southern Africa through the expansion of (primarily) White capital is a very tangible opinion across the region.

The Emergence of the MDC

The MDC is the best known and arguably the most successful SDI in the southern African region. It involves the governments of South Africa and Mozambique working in partnership with both domestic and international private sector. To date the two governments have created the necessary environment for the establishment of physical infrastructure linking the two neighbouring countries. The MDC is essentially a transport axis between Gauteng province, the industrial hub of South Africa and Maputo. This transport route was particularly popular during the 1970s when forty per cent of the exports from Gauteng province went through the nearby port of Maputo, which is 160km closer than the alternative South African port of Durban. The 1980s however, witnessed a sharp decline in the use of the route. In 1975 the port of Maputo handled over 6 million tons of South African cargo a year but by 1988 this had plummeted to 250,000 tons due to South Africa's destabilisation activities and the protracted civil war in Mozambique.

The MDC was designed as a mixed industrial and agri-tourism SDI. According to the South African Department of Trade and Industry (DTI), the MDC is designed in order to have beneficial socio-economic effects for South Africa, Mozambique, Swaziland, Botswana and Zimbabwe. However, thus far and for a long time to come, the benefits will be primarily confined to South Africa and Mozambique, the two countries directly linked by the corridor. The two countries have developed industrial relations based on supposed mutual economic interests, with South Africa being the initial and main beneficiary whilst Mozambique is to, if all goes according to plan, benefit from the anticipated spread-effects. It appears that in spite of the asymmetric relationship, there is a clear understanding by both governments about the common benefits to be derived from the project.

South African interests in the MDC are twofold. First, the government wants reliable access to the port of Maputo. Second, and perhaps more importantly, Pretoria also seeks to develop the economically marginal and impoverished Mpumalanga province. From its inception, the MDC has been expected by the government's spatial planners to unlock the industrial development potential of this province, which historically has been neglected by the state for political and security reasons. Also, the Mpumalanga province has been badly affected by the decline of the trade route to the sea during the Mozambican civil war, which ended in the early 1990s. Mozambique, on the other hand, has sought to develop the Maputo province, which is its core economic region and inhabited by over fifty per cent of the country's population.

The historical timing of the launch of the MDC was ideal. The demise of apartheid and the end of the civil war in Mozambique unlocked significant investment capital that immediately became available to the region. It could also be said that for South Africa, the corridor project would provide a sense of indirect moral restitution for its part in the destabilising civil war in Mozambique. It would become an important symbol of a new relationship that would fulfil the important clauses of the Nkomati Accord signed during the apartheid era. Key social events like the marriage between the then president of South Africa, Nelson Mandela and the former first lady of Mozambique, Graça Machel, indirectly helped bilateral discussions that led to the concretisation of the MDC and also symbolised, in a highly personalised fashion, the new post-apartheid relationship between Mozambique and South Africa.

Before considering the significance of the MDC in southern Africa, we provide a very brief description of the corridor (detailed historical development has been done in sufficient detail elsewhere, see Söderbaum and Taylor, chapter 1; Mitchell, 1998; Tevera and Chimhowu, 2000). Technically, the MDC is based on six key activities: the 505km toll road from Witbank to Maputo; the upgrading of the port of Maputo; the railway lines to the port of Maputo; improved border facilities and management; industrial investments in various sectors to boost exports, such as Mozal; and local level programmes to spread the benefits of the corridor (see more details in De Beer and Arkwright, chapter 2).

Geographically, the Maputo Corridor consists of the following components: a primary corridor area composed of the main transport and communication infrastructure (road, rail and telecommunications) between Witbank and Maputo and including the main urban centres; a secondary corridor consisting of administratively defined areas immediately adjacent to the primary area; tertiary resource nodes and feeder links; the Phalaborwa sub-corridor; and the Inhambane sub-corridor. It is evident from this geographical definition that the South African government perceives the MDC as being both about the development of an efficient and quick transport network to the sea from the Gauteng province as well as about the economic development of the micro-regional space economy.

The MDC and Uneven Development

At first glance, the MDC has brought benefits in the form of numerous projects and jobs to the region that it traverses. By 2001 about 6,200 jobs had been created through road construction, of which 1,100 were in Mozambique. Furthermore, up to 9,000 workers were employed, of whom seventy per cent were Mozambicans, during the construction of the Mozal aluminium smelter (see Hentz, chapter 7). When fully functional the Mozal alone should have created over 8,000 jobs. However, most of the jobs for Mozambicans are low skilled.

The infrastructural improvements envisaged are expected to transform the space economy of the corridor region, while increased revenue from taxes and levies will accrue to both the South African and Mozambican states (see Ngwenya and Taylor, chapter 6). There is some evidence that the employment generated has boosted the incomes of the people along the corridor and as the corridor traffic has increased, some of the towns such as Nelspruit have experienced increased rates of population and spatial growth.

Regional investment in the productive sector by South African companies in partnership with other international and national firms has also helped Mozambique to increase exports and hence export earnings. Certainly, the Mozal plant has provided substantial earnings in taxes and dividends to the Mozambican state (see Hentz, chapter 7). Similarly, increased port, road and rail traffic may well increase the government's share of the earnings, although it remains questionable whether Mozambican earnings from the N4 toll road will offset its losses of road tax receipts. However, while the private sector investment as the engine of growth has been accepted as the guiding principle in the MDC, the benefits that are accruable to the ordinary South Africans and Mozambicans in the Mpumalanga and Maputo provinces have been limited (Baptista-Lundin and Taylor, chapter 8). Indeed, the MDC reveals some of the flaws in the SDI strategy. For example, many of the jobs that have been created are temporary and are related to construction projects (Söderbaum and Taylor, chapter 4). Furthermore, the MDC has not yet succeeded in integrating historically disadvantaged Black communities, especially in Mpumalanga. The MDC has thus far demonstrated two biases: an urban bias and a strong racial bias in the ownership of economic assets. The racial bias is demonstrated, for instance, by the fact that most of the approximately 1,000 tourist facilities in Mpumalanga are owned by Whites.

As a matter of fact, the MDC has been unable to achieve its aims thus far because of the tensions inherent in its goals. When faced with the two goals of attracting investment and empowering local communities, the former has received a much higher priority by those involved in the SDI process (see Söderbaum and Taylor, chapter 4). Because most of the investment is being driven by the private sector, this pattern is unlikely to change without significant government intervention. For South Africa, Van Zuydam (1998) has shown that the redistributive dimension of the SDIs may be questionable if current investment trends continue whereby locations within the former "White" areas are preferred by investors, leaving the former Black homelands to look to the state for investment, something which due to the economic model adopted by the South African government is questionable.

Furthermore, the MDC as it has so far developed cements the dominance of South Africa. For example, Driver and De Barros (2000) expect more than ninety per cent of the revenue from tolls to come from the South African side of the border. Moreover, out of the 29,000 tons passing through the border post, about 26,000 tons went from South Africa to Mozambique while only 3,000 tons of goods went from Mozambique to South Africa. This raises questions about the uneven developmental impacts of corridors within southern Africa due to existing trade imbalances and the historically asymmetric relationship that characterises the whole region. It is clear that South Africa is the powerful and dominant partner in the two-country-partnership and the unequal partnership and dominance almost certainly explains the differentials in the progress made on the South African and Mozambican sections of the corridor (see Baptista-Lundin and Taylor, chapter 8). Most of the developments have been concentrated on the South African side where strong institutional structures related to the project are in place.

The MDC may also have a polarising effect inside Mozambique itself where more than 70 per cent of the industrial activity is confined to the regions of Beira and Maputo, which cover less than 40 per cent of the national territory (Weimer, 1996). There are, therefore, renewed fears that uneven development in Mozambique will be amplified as the economically active labour force are drawn to the MDC area in search of employment and other income generating opportunities. This may result in a southward migration of people and other factors of production, especially capital. For Mozambique, this may bring more problems: already, there is an exodus of people to the coastal zones and the city of Maputo in particular (see Baptista-Lundin and Taylor, chapter 8).

The MDC and SADC: An Uneasy Relationship?

The ostensible objective of the SADC is to harmonise production in the region and to facilitate deeper economic co-operation and regional integration on the basis of balance, equity and mutual benefit. This is to be achieved by combining the compartmentalised economies and fragmented markets of the community through the relaxation of national tariffs. The spatial structure of the predominantly extractive regional economy, which has become the mainstay of national markets, has created dismembered spatial entities characterised by tenuous and difficult transport and communication links.

On paper the MDC seems to resonate with the SADC's aim to move towards regional co-operation in all economic sectors as well as the free movement of factors of production, trade and investment across national borders. However, it still remains to be seen whether the MDC can realise this desire. The region itself has had a protracted history of regional disputes and discord that can inhibit the smooth operation of transnational SDIs in southern Africa. Furthermore, the differences in capacity and ability to collect and process information can lead to differential commitment levels with respect to the formation and operation of SDIs. The high transaction costs involved due to the large distances between the participating countries may also inhibit the smooth operation of the corridors.

By implementing the corridor project outside the framework of SADC, South Africa and Mozambique have evoked the unwritten principle of variable geometry and the multi-speed approach to regional co-operation (Tsie, 1996). This allows member states to go ahead with programmes of common interest without waiting for the laggards to participate. South Africa has already done this in the case of the Lesotho Highlands Water Project and with Mozambique concerning the various energy projects. Sooner or later, bilateral corridors that exclude other regional members will divide the regional body and this is why, despite the initial success, there are several flaws in the SDI paradigm and a fear that variable geometry and multi-speedism may actually undermine regional equity and increase the flow of people to the corridor in search of opportunities (Venter, 1995).

Having said that, countries like Swaziland and Zimbabwe, which have increased their sugar and coal exports through the MDC, have already shown an interest in the project. In fact, between 1996 and 1998, a million tons of sugar from Zimbabwe and Swaziland were handled by the Maputo port, bringing revenue to the Mozambican economy close to US$17 million in the form of direct and indirect incomes, port duties and various levies. Zimbabwe constructed a railway line to join the corridor from Beitbridge and Botswana has indicated to the Beira Corridor Group that it has no more interest in that route. Botswana is already operating, with Namibia, the Trans-Kalahari Corridor, with its outlet at Walvis Bay on the Atlantic coast. Linking this up to the MDC on the Indian Ocean coast seems logical and the preferred trade route. The economic meltdown unfolding since early 2000 in Zimbabwe may however drastically reduce the expected boom in export activity along the MDC. It is particularly the latter case that underscores the importance of regional political stability in underpinning the success of spatial integration of the region.

Mistry (2001) is correct in asserting that failed integration is explained by the conflicting disposition among African states to remain politically separate (keeping their state sovereignty and room for manoeuvre by the elites) while at the same time being convinced of the need to achieve economic integration, but at "arms length". As a way out of this contradiction, SADC has tacitly tolerated the development of sub-regions and micro-regions within the broader southern African region.

The multi-speed approach, as exemplified by the MDC, has brought Mozambique and South Africa together, but there are fears that this tends to undermine regional unity as it introduces sub- and micro-regions within the macro-region. In the case of Africa and more specifically the SADC region, signs of the divisive effects of the variable geometry and multi-speed approach are apparent already as countries identify areas where they wish to be closer to each other. In the case of SADC it means that as a result of the way the regional grouping has been evolving, with the admittance of questionable new members (e.g. the Democratic Republic of the Congo), there are now only certain members that have close historical ties. It is easier to achieve integration for these countries compared to the rest. For example, South Africa may find it easier to integrate with members of the Southern African Customs Union (SACU), comprising South Africa, Botswana, Lesotho, Swaziland and Namibia, because of their historical ties. One could argue that the manner in which SADC is evolving will hinder the emergence of other SDIs in the region that are modelled along the MDC concept.

Conclusion

The MDC is one of the few SDIs in the southern Africa region that can claim to have had some distinct impacts on the regional space economy. From the point of view of SADC's regional co-operation goals the MDC is an initiative which is worth supporting: the goals of the MDC do seem to resonate with SADC's aim to facilitate regional economic co-operation. However, the MDC's experience in South Africa and Mozambique shows that while economic growth has occurred in the corridor region, its distribution has been skewed in favour of the more developed areas and the more well to do population groups. Also, there has been limited spread and trickle-down effects to generate the anticipated development impulses in the lagging areas and this seems to defeat one of the overarching goals of the MDC.

It still remains to be seen whether a plethora of development zones, as espoused in the SDI concept, will transform the national space economies within the region in the manner that the MDC aims to do in South Africa and Mozambique. The limited success of the MDC largely depends on a combination of unique economic and geographic factors. However, the extent to which the MDC is replicable elsewhere in the region is questionable and needs careful consideration. Clearly, both historical and geographical factors provided a unique setting that is difficult to replicate elsewhere in the SADC region. It is not clear whether the spatially focused economic investment approach, driven by private investment, will be able to trigger development in the other targeted areas nor avoid effective economic (or even political) polarisation within the SADC region.

Chapter 4

The Role of the State in the Maputo Development Corridor*

Fredrik Söderbaum and Ian Taylor

Southern Africa is currently experiencing a profound transformation. We are witnessing a complex and often turbulent process in which regionalism and regionalisation interact with other processes of change, most notably globalisation, the post-Cold War milieu and, of course, post-apartheid regional transformations, structural adjustment and the restructuring of the nation-state. In line with most other regions of the world, southern Africa is also experiencing a (re-)emergence of various types of cross-border micro-regions, most notably the much-hyped Maputo Development Corridor (MDC).

One of the keys to understanding this new turbulence is to look at what is happening to the constitutive elements of the old order, above all the state. It is difficult to dispute that states take part and often seek to push globalisation. According to one influential line of thinking, the state has become the disciplining spokesperson of transnational capital, a "transmission belt" for economic globalisation. This is in contrast to the conceptualisation of the state as a "buffer", protecting the domestic economy from harmful exogenous influences (Cox, 1996b). Yet, in a globalised world, with territories more and more integrated, the buffer concept appears increasingly redundant. Rather, an intermediary position, where the state mediates between local interests and external capital seems the most apposite strategy to pursue, certainly preferable to an emasculated state reduced to little more than the facilitator for international capital. Clearly, given that states are more and more deeply embedded in the global economy (and since autocentric development is untenable in the context of globalisation), the role of the state in promoting and facilitating development needs serious interrogation.

Taking this point of departure, this chapter seeks to assess the role of the state in the promotion of development in the MDC. Has the rolling back of the state, which is concomitant with orthodox liberalisation policies, meant that the state is now best understood as a "transmission belt" for transnational capital? If so, what does this imply for developmental ambitions within the MDC? Or should the role of the state in the MDC instead be understood as a project to construct a "developmental state" along the lines pursued in East Asia, which have been relatively successful in serving as mediating actors regarding the power and impact of external capital and behaving as promoters of quite phenomenal development?

The concept of the state as a transmission belt rests on the policies adopted by liberalising countries. Trade liberalisation, structural adjustment programmes and the elimination of capital controls can, if advanced too far, emasculate the state and deny administrations the ability to formulate and pursue defensive fiscal and monetary policies. Despite their political and economic differences, both South Africa and Mozambique have adopted neo-liberal policies that fit with the norms advocated by the international financial institutions (IFIs), global capital, their main Northern trading partners and donors. Both countries are emerging, to varying degrees, from years of civil strife and economic decline (or collapse). In doing so, the state elites of both countries have based their developmental models on a gamble on investment and "going for growth". Clearly, in the absence of sufficient domestic savings and the monumental developmental tasks in front of them, capital must be sourced from somewhere. Given the decline in overall aid to the continent and the massive debt facing Mozambique, funds from donors and/or further borrowing cannot be relied upon for generating sufficient capital. Attracting external investment then is seen as the key to promoting development in both countries. This is seen as the realities that need to be faced. From this has sprung the belief that 'there is no alternative' to, as one critic put it, 'the ceding to the market the determination of economic performance' (Weeks, 1996: 117). Such policies do indeed render the state as a transmission belt for international capital. Much of the policies pursued within the MDC advance such a proposition, with problematic results, as will be demonstrated.

However, it is simplistic to dichotomise between the two extremes of either transmission belt or buffer state. In the case of Mozambique and South Africa, the endogenous policies of the past were disastrous: both apartheid and an overly ambitious attempt at crafting a command economy were locally determined. Clearly, it is of limited use to see "the state" as an inexorable tool against the outside. History has sufficiently demonstrated that harmful exogenous influences may pale to insignificance against the destructive talents of endogenous actors. Furthermore, the MDC project has arisen within the context not only of changes in the global political economy, but also within the milieu of a political opening in both countries that has meant a retreat by each state within the political realm. Coupled with outside forces that press for a "dual transition" (read: rolling back) that equally encompasses the economic, the role of the state in development strategies is an area of deep contestation.

It is important to emphasise that the construction of the MDC has involved (at least) two interactive processes: top-down and institution-building strategies, on the one hand, and bottom-up processes and the re-scaling of identities and social relations, on the other hand. Through this distinction we seek to transcend the tendency in the debate to exaggerate formal institution-building. In this context it is important to recognise that the present attempt to construct the MDC builds upon the historical region that has existed between southern Mozambique and eastern South Africa for many decades and very often has occurred "beneath the nation-state" (see Söderbaum and Taylor, chapter 1). Notwithstanding, the mere size and magnitude of the top-down MDC project makes it of crucial importance, and it will therefore be an important component of our analysis.

The chapter is structured as follows. In the next section, we consider the inconsistency of the underlying development paradigm and strategy that the MDC is founded upon. The problem is that whereas the MDC is officially held to be about "development" the "really existing" project is about facilitating private and bankable investment projects, often of gigantic proportions. Such interrogation leads us to a fundamental focus of this volume, namely exactly "whose corridor" is being created? Is the MDC for "the people", or is it primarily to facilitate and attract capital? As a means of shedding light on such questions, we analyse the partnerships with the private sector that the MDC programme is supposed to develop, and with whom and for whom such partnerships are created. In the final section the perspective is broadened, and we discuss whether the current restricted role of the state in the MDC and the "big-bang" approach associated with the MDC can work.

Development vs. Bankable Investment

The MDC is a major investment initiative that aims to maximise infrastructure and social investment and provide access to global capital, facilitate regional markets and regional economic integration within a holistic, participatory and environmentally sustainable approach to development. As elaborated upon in detail by De Beer and Arkwright (chapter 2), the MDC contains a very comprehensive investment portfolio, centred around some anchor and key sector infrastructural and industrial investment projects, such as the Mozal I and II (US$2.3 billion) (see Hentz, chapter 7); Maputo Iron and Steel Project (US$1.5 billion); Pande/Temane Gas (US$250 million); the Witbank-Maputo N4 toll road (US$400 million) (see Ngwenya and Taylor, chapter 6); the rehabilitation of the port of Maputo (US$85 million); the southern Mozambique rail network (US$70 million); and the Ressano Garcia/Komatipoort border post (US$1.5 million).

This leads us to argue that the MDC paradigm is predicated on a "big-bang" approach built around short-term, capital-intensive and large-scale investment, with a minimal degree of state involvement. In spite of its label as a *development* corridor, the MDC approach is built around the key goal to "crowd in" private *investments*. It is only to a minor extent a planning exercise (i.e. the allocation of public resources). Basically, the MDC is about "investment attraction" and "market guidance", where the state *suggests* opportunities to the private sector, with the *hope* that this will create jobs. Furthermore, as noted above, these investments are of gigantic proportions, and therefore extremely reliant on foreign investment capital, at least in Mozambique. This overall strategy has involved very little input from the affected populations. Indeed, such "big-bang" capital-intensive projects provoke serious questions related to what type of development is being promoted in the MDC, whose corridor is it, and who stands to benefit?

Ironically, the MDC's prospectus *does* include developmental commitments and references to environmental awareness. For instance, MDC's key objectives (3 and 4) are supposed to: maximise social development, employment opportunities and increase the participation of historically disadvantaged communities; and ensure sustainability by developing policy, strategies and frameworks that ensure a holistic, participatory and environmentally sustainable approach to development, respectively. Furthermore, the MDC's 'Strategic Context' and 'Vision' states that:

> The re-establishment of the [Witbank-Maputo] axis will significantly enhance the underlying conditions for development along its entire length...The development corridor will also present opportunities to address the important (corridor and wider regional area) issues of sustainability (natural resource use, refined industrial processes etc.), poverty and access to basic needs and social services (DBSA, 2001b).

Indeed, the World Bank's deputy chief resident in South Africa asserted that 'the Corridor must be seen as a means to an end, and that end is poverty alleviation' (*Cape Times*, 11 August, 1997). However, such developmental impulses are profoundly compromised by the diverse and often contradictory manner by which projects are being implemented on the ground. Indeed, there are indications that there is a dislocation between many of the plans, and how they are being implemented, undermining the expressed developmental agenda behind the MDC's genesis and raising important questions regarding exactly for whom is the micro-region being constructed. Attempting to understand the negative trajectories that a number of the MDC's projects have stimulated casts some light on this fundamental issue.

At the heart of any interrogation of the MDC lies the macro-economic vision upon which it is predicated, which, like many development projects currently being promoted in the South are based on common sense understandings of what constitutes "good" policies (Klak and Myers, 1997). The neo-liberal forces behind the Corridor's inception can only push for further privatisation and the rolling back of state involvement (Torp and Rekve, 1998). What we are suggesting here is that the state is in danger of being relegated to becoming simply a transmission belt for transnational capital. Such strategies cast everything within a profit-seeking and "bankable" framework, which allows very little space for tackling the social and ecological implications that the various projects engender.

It is difficult to dispute that the MDC is designed first and foremost for "big business", and local participation is more by coincidence rather than a guiding component of the MDC paradigm and strategy as such. By this we mean that the

SDI strategy and the MDC in particular is founded on a capital-intensive, big business and top-down development strategy, with the real intention to increase export growth and gross domestic product (GDP) rather than people-centred development. In this light, the MDC appears to be basically an investment initiative of gigantic proportions, to some extent resembling the old capital-intensive, "big-bang" approaches prevalent in the 1950s and 1960s, but minus the guiding role of the state in mediating between the interests of capital and labour and, in the contemporary world, between the transnational and national. Holistic, environmentally sustainable and people-centred development aspects (MDC objective 4) are difficult to discover in any practical implementation of the MDC.

In contrast to its stated objectives, the "actually existing" MDC is based on a narrow and almost naïve strategy on how to promote economic development (or rather, growth), whereby development is believed to arise more or less automatically as a result of the implementation of bankable mega-projects i.e. infrastructure, aluminium smelters, iron and steel projects and so on. Needless to say, given their size, these mega-projects are bound to have some effects on development, or at least on economic growth. For instance, the Mozal project is estimated to double the export earnings of Mozambique (*Agencia Informação Moçambique*, Maputo, 9 October, 2000; see also Hentz, chapter 7). However, the relevance of an initiative, that on average involves a cost of US$200,000 per job in a context of labour-surplus economies and mass unemployment, can certainly be problematised. In late 1999, investments worth US$ four billion had been secured, but these projects are only estimated to be able to create 12,000 jobs. In our view it is quite clear that the MDC and the investment strategies being advanced have the danger of conforming with neo-liberal trends towards "jobless growth". For instance, 9,000 workers were employed during the construction of the US$1.3 billion Mozal project, but it will only create 743 permanent jobs in itself (BusinessMap, 2000: 37). Available evidence suggests that the most important motive for Mozal is *not* to create jobs but to use it as a "show case" to demonstrate that mega-projects can be viably undertaken in Mozambique and thereby increase the profile and credit rating of the region (ibid.). In such light, to whom does the MDC then belong?

Whose Corridor?

A host of problems arising as a consequence of the "big-bang" approach, with its emphasis on the privatisation of state functions and the premature "retreat" of central and provincial government, need discussing. As far as institutions are concerned, such processes have resulted in unclear responsibilities between central and provincial institutions as well as between national, provincial and local actors, who all seem to have different understandings of the content of the MDC strategy. Certainly, although the MDC is well-known, especially internationally, its content is not at the local level.[1] There are severe institutional constraints and low capacities at provincial and local levels which are a direct consequence of the minimalist approach to institutions taken by the two central governments. This prevents effective implementation as well as monitoring of overall development effects. All these problems are particularly evident on the Mozambican side of the border, where it is not altogether clear whether the central government has actually grasped the MDC concept and the strategy behind it. The regime in Maputo has thus far demonstrated a lack of commitment and has devoted very limited institutional resources for its functioning, reflected by the fact that the Maputo Corridor unit in the Department of Transport in Maputo (GPZ) is more or less non-functioning, with very limited staff and almost non-existent resources. Indeed, the authors observed that the unit, situated on the top-floor of the dilapidated Department of Transport building in Maputo, had one computer and only one (harassed) member of staff in the entire office. The overlooking of institution-building is further illustrated by the failure to establish the Maputo Corridor Company (MCC) in Mozambique, even though the MCC is supposed to be part of the overall decentralisation strategy and also the mechanism to integrate local communities and local private economic actors into the MDC process (see Söderbaum, chapter 5).[2]

Furthermore, as mentioned above, the "big-bang", top-down approach impulses and the concomitant privatisation of everyday life is extremely problematic to implement in the context of an impoverished part of the world and the projects advanced thus far appear to be totally inappropriate to the kind of investment that the region—and specifically Mozambique—needs. This can be illustrated by mentioning the impact the MDC will have on the capital's water supply. Over sixty per cent of Maputo's residents live in absolute poverty (Rodolfo, 1998: 8), and the city's low-income neighbourhoods' access to potable water is very poor, particularly so during the rainy season, when pit latrines overflow, thus sparking regular cholera outbreaks. Not only is the water available in the poor residential areas limited, much of it is frequently contaminated. Access to this vital life source however is going to be further compromised by one of the mega-projects of the MDC, the Maputo Iron and Steel Project, which requires fifty-seven million litres of water per day. Together with another South African investment—the 250,000 ton Mozal aluminium smelter—nearly forty per cent of the Maputo region's total water resources are to be devoted to servicing these industries. The amount of water left (120 million cubic metres) is simply 'insufficient to supply the city [of Maputo] even at the present medium levels of consumption' (National Directorate of Local Administration, Mozambique 'The Structure Plan for Greater Maputo', cited in *Sunday Independent*, Johannesburg, 10 October, 1999).

Ecological security within the Mozambican sector of the micro-region is further undermined by the discharge of effluents from the two South African projects into a bay already saturated with other pollutants derived from an inadequate system to treat and dispose of human waste (*Sunday Independent*, Johannesburg, 10 October 1999). As if this was not enough, magnetite slurry and steel slag being transported to the Iron and Steel Project by locomotives are ecologically hazardous and require specialist care and management. Unfortunately, this management capacity is not currently available in Mozambique. Indeed, this inability to treat such environmentally perilous material is symptomatic of the poor manner in which ecological concerns have been managed within the micro-region, particularly on the Mozambican side. According to one report:

> As part of the [Structure Plan for Greater Maputo] environmental analyses were conducted on domestic energy, sanitation and drainage, and water quality. All five reports revealed inadequate and ineffective management of environmental and natural resources for their long-term, sustainable uses (*Sunday Independent*, Johannesburg, 10 October, 1999).

If ecological security remains unprioritised and the welfare of the residents of Maputo a side-issue to the concerns of the investors ('cheap electricity and tax initiatives...by the Mozambican government' according to Mozal chairman, Rob Barbour, quoted in *Business Day*, Johannesburg, 4 October 1999), fundamental questions need to be asked regarding the ownership of the micro-region and whose "development" is being privileged.

Similarly, issues surrounding gender equity and accessibility to any developmental spin-offs that may accrue from the MDC remain unproblematised. Perhaps the most contentious issue in this regard is the N4 toll road and the privatisation of formerly publicly accessible transport routes (see Ngwenya and Taylor, chapter 6). This has already provoked severe tensions between local communities and the investors involved in the project. Initially, rural local women were chased off the N4 for trying to sell fruit to travellers, something they have done for decades.[3] With the increasing traffic flows along this route, the impoverished women felt that they had a right to try and make a living this way. However, the local council demanded that such activities be licensed and formalised and the women moved to a planned "mini-market". Local women interviewed felt that this would deprive them of potential customers (*Mail and Guardian*, Johannesburg, 15 June, 1998).

Consultation with local communities over such issues seems minimal and is only really enacted when effected local inhabitants complain, leading to what one analysis of emerging regionalisms in southern Africa refers to as the SDI's 'democratic deficit' (Shaw, 2000). Indeed, women have lost out thus far in a number of projects related to the MDC. The majority of tenders to build the N4 toll route were awarded to male-managed businesses and according to one report, only one women-owned company was granted a contract. The imbalance in female involvement in the micro-region's construction sparked the (South African) Commission on Gender Equality to gauge the empowerment of Black women along the Corridor, with one member remarking that 'sadly, the only industry that appears to be working for women is sex work that has sprung up along the highway, which is unfortunately accompanied by the increase in HIV and AIDS' (Colleen Lowe-Morna, quoted by *African Eye News Service*, Nelspruit, 14 February, 1999).

Partnerships: With Whom?

As mentioned previously, one crucial component of the MDC programme is to create partnerships with the private sector. This has lead to the emergence of so-called public-private partnerships (PPPs), which are mechanisms for involving the private sector and broadening the ownership base, especially in order to enhance the delivery of infrastructure and other state functions. The Witbank-Maputo N4 toll road is the most comprehensive PPP within the MDC project (see Ngwenya and Taylor, chapter 6). Other PPPs include the one-stop border post at Ressano Garcia/Nkomati and the Maputo port. The PPPs imply a commercialisation and/or privatisation of conventional state functions and public goods. In addition, the Mozambican state is in a rapid process of outright privatisation of infrastructure such as roads (*Agencia Informação Moçambique*, Maputo, 13, January, 2000). In Mozambique this means a retreat from one extreme to another: the state has now abandoned its heavy *dirigiste* position to one of abdication in involvement in the economy. An outspoken "market paradigm" rules investment decisions in the MDC project, with the mediating influence of the state being absent at most levels.

What is emerging is not a partnership between state and capital in the service of the public good, but rather a *deal* between the political elite and transnational capital, supported by the IFIs and the donor community, to rush headlong into liberalisation (Hanlon, 1991). In doing so, the pay-off is predicated on the belief that "development" will inexorably proceed growth—in short, "trickle-down" theory. According to this dominant paradigm, good governance is defined as *less* government. Indeed, as Hanlon notes, 'the hegemony of this view is now absolute; even relatively progressive Northern government ministers, officials and legislators (and many in the South) accept unquestionably that "good governance" is synonymous with IMF structural adjustment policies' (Hanlon, 1999: 32). In the case of the MDC this is taken even one step further: the state is reduced to an investment promotion agency to provide technical support in the privatisation process (Hanlon, 1996). That is, the role of the state is simply to boost new bankable and commercially viable investment projects, most often of gigantic proportions. In accepting this ideology the state becomes the disciplining spokesman of global economic forces, a transmission belt for economic globalisation, rather than a mediating influence seeking to craft beneficial partnerships that promote development.

Clearly, it would be illusionary to think of the state in Mozambique acting to "protect" the citizenry. Its legitimacy has always been suspect and, perhaps except for a *brief* period in the immediate post-independence period, has acted according to type, namely, having been born and bred as the instrument of international capital, the state has a function that has remained largely constant. In this light, the retreat by the Mozambican state from its grandiose development-building ambitions is a return to normalcy and not some aberration. Protests about the "abandonment" of socialism ring rather hollow in such an analysis (Cahen, 1993). Having said that, regarding the communication between the state and "civil society", there now seems to be a greater willingness to forgo popular consent and dialogue, remarkable in that Mozambique has gone through an ostensible "democratisation" process. This of course is not to romanticise Frelimo's relationship with civil society: tensions have long existed and autocratic rule has long staked out this association—the strains between state and citizenry over the Corridor may be but a continuation of the alienation experienced between state and citizen that stretches back to the colonial period and, as has been intimated, marked out much of Frelimo's rule post-independence. Yet, and this needs saying, the current development thinking of the Mozambican state in practice lacks a concern for the victims of structural change. This helps us understand why the people living in the Corridor have not been consulted about the MDC's strategy, nor integrated into decision-making (see Söderbaum, chapter 5; Baptista-Lundin and Taylor, chapter 8). This, combined with the long-standing practice by Frelimo of adopting top-down directives with little democratic input, produces what may be seen as a democratic deficit, particularly on the Mozambican side but similar problems arise in South Africa as well. The comment by a transport economist from the Mozambican Ministry of Transport and Communications that the people simply 'have to get used to paying' is indicative of this mind-set by many within the Frelimo state.[4]

"Big-Bang" Development: Can It Work?

This chapter has been critical of the developmental impulses—or lack of them—that seem to characterise the MDC. It does not however willy-nilly dismiss private investment within the initiatives currently reconfiguring the region, nor does it dismiss out of hand many of the features of the SDIs. For instance, the emphasis on rapid implementation and the streamlining of bureaucratic barriers to investment, as well as the notion of one-stop border formalities and integrated consulting centres all act to stimulate investment *and* lift the weight of often capricious officialdom from the backs of citizens. This can only be a good thing. The rapidity that characterises much of the MDC's operations can also be positive in that it creates space for considerable innovation and experimentation in directing and then evaluating projects. The parsimonious nature of much of the top-level structures provides a flexibility that may well be constrained in other, more traditional regional co-operation initiatives in Africa (Söderbaum, chapter 5). Furthermore, the active involvement of the private sector in projects can stimulate local-level development. However, this needs active guidance from state bodies in order to promote small and medium enterprise engagement, as well as mediate between the interest of capital and labour. Differently expressed, development and poverty alleviation do not just "happen" automatically as a result of commercial private investment projects. Specific contractual obligations to involve local partners on the ground, particularly those managed by and with a strong labour component comprised of disadvantaged persons, such as indigenous Africans and women, would be vital to any such positive spin-offs from private sector involvement.

The "market" cannot be left to its own devices if development and empowerment within the MDC (and indeed other SDIs) is to be realised. Our analysis suggests that the SDI methodology in general and the MDC strategy in particular in many ways is, if not a dead-end, at least the wrong way. If the state's role is limited to simply being a transmission belt for transnational investor capital, the capacity to monitor and also resolve the social implications of the MDC is greatly reduced. This has profound implications for the *developmental* potential of the project. In order to recapture the initiative and help guide development in the micro-region, it is imperative that the state goes beyond the present SDI-methodology whereby government is reduced to little more than acting as an investment promotion agency facilitating "big-bang" projects.

Under present circumstances there is no convincing evidence that the state will be able to build a participatory and people-centred development in the MDC, which works hand in hand with civil actors. One main obstacle is the retreat of the state and the minimalist view on governance institutions and mechanisms. The role of the state has been inexorably reduced to facilitating private, commercially viable investment projects and not much else. Certainly, there are no institutions that can facilitate dialogue with bottom-up forces in society. In fact there is even some evidence that the state has no ambition to sustain a people-centred development. For instance, the Deputy Director General responsible for the SDI process at the DTI has asserted that 'SDIs are a proven means of giving government more job-creating bang for its very limited bucks [and the strategy] is too important...to be derailed by vested interests and narrow agendas' (*Mail and Guardian*, 7 November 1997). It is all too easy to dismiss concerns expressed by civil society as that of 'vested interests', yet in doing so bottom-up forces may be marginalised and ignored, which can only lead to problems in the future.

We are arguing that the fast-track approach of the SDI-methodology is not only a short-track approach but in fact may be counter-productive. There is no escape from the fact that a people-centred development must, by its very definition, develop mechanisms that work hand in hand with those on the ground who are most likely to be affected by initiatives such as SDI projects (Emmett 2000). At present, this can only be located within the state, acting in a mediating role. As Midgley puts it:

> If the critical problems of mass poverty and deprivation in the Third World are to be dealt with, concerted action by the state will be needed. Local people do not have the resources to solve these problems through their own efforts alone...Participation is highly desirable but the poor cannot survive on rhetoric and idealism (Midgley, 1986: 158-159).

Clearly, this is not to romanticise the state's intentions or, in the context of South Africa and (particularly) Mozambique, capacity. For any developmental state project to work, capacity is obviously crucial and, at present, is lacking at a variety of levels in both states under consideration. But, capacity-building is not impossible and seems eminently feasible, indeed vital, if a more active role for the state in crafting a working partnership with capital is to be realised. It is suggested that rather than funding projects to advance further liberalisation and the rolling back of the state, the donor community would be better advised funding capacity-building programmes with the target of facilitating a reinvigorated state that can act within some intermediary position, serving to mediate between local interests and external capital.

A reactivated role for the state, in tandem with popular interests, needs to engage with the MDC process, rather than allow capital an overly privileged role. Recognising that 'governments on their own are unlikely to act to promote the public good unless pressured by their constituencies' (Cheru, 1997: 219) but that 'state-society synergy lies at the heart of developmental success' (Evans, 1996: 1035), a reformulated role for both the state and civil actors appears intelligent. It is not enough to predicate the micro-region simply around "growth" and hope that empowerment will occur. Only if this fundamental problem is concretely addressed can the impulses currently animating the micro-region be deployed in the service of those who most need them. Whether this is possible in an epoch where neo-liberalism is currently hegemonic and where the role of the state is viewed with intense suspicion is open to question. But, as other experiences have shown, for instance, in Botswana (Samatar, 1999), the either/or of transmission belt or buffer can be overcome and the orthodoxy that the market is the be-all and end-all of decisions on the potentiality of development projects be avoided.

Accepting this, there is a very important role that the South African and Mozambican states are failing to play. This is namely, selective interventions in order to guide and harness the market to promote local, national and regional developmental goals. Such a developmental state would, for instance, seek out a partnership role with capital to foster the development of intermediate and capital goods. This intervention would serve to yield different investment results than otherwise would occur following the transmission belt scenario, as well as mediating for a true partnership with capital that would provide the means for the MDC to serve the broader interests of its people, rather than privileging private investors and international capital. 'The fundamental issue is the form, quality and scope of state intervention' (Tsie, 1996: 94). Noting that the MDC is the flagship of the SDI programme, a rethinking of the facilitating role of the state in these various micro-regions appears urgently required.

Notes

* An earlier and more detailed version of this chapter appeared as Fredrik Söderbaum and Ian Taylor 'Transmission Belt for Transnational Capital or Facilitator for Development? Problematising the Role of the State in the Maputo Development Corridor', *Journal of Modern African Studies*, vol. 39, no. 4, December 2001: 675-695. The permission to publish is gratefully acknowledged.

1. Interview with Milissão Nuvunga, lecturer at the *Instituto Superior de Relações Internacionais* (ISRI), Maputo, 7 April 2000.

2. Interview with David Arkwright, South African Project Manager of MDC, Nelspruit, 12 April 2000.
3. Interviews with informal traders outside Nelspruit, 3 April 2000.
4. Interview with Francisca Soares, Project Manager, Mozambican Ministry of Transport and Communications, Maputo, 10 April 2000.

Chapter 5

Governance in the Maputo Development Corridor

Fredrik Söderbaum

The Spatial Development Initiative (SDI) programme is currently the most distinct form of policy-driven micro-regionalism in southern Africa. SDIs are built on a particular type of decision-making and implementation procedure (i.e. governance), consisting of core features, such as political champions, a minimal institutional structure, fast-tracking of design and implementation and a special relationship towards provincial governments and—at least in theory—local communities. The purpose of this chapter is to critically assess the specific and intriguing modes of governance in the MDC, with a particular focus on the patterns of inclusion and exclusion.

The analysis takes its point of departure from the new regionalism approach (NRA). As outlined in the introduction, the NRA emphasises the notion that regionalism must be placed within its particular historical context as well as related to the current transformation of a globalising world. Similar to globalisation, it is argued that regionalisation is often an instrument to supplement, enhance or reconfigure the role of the state and the power of government in an interdependent world (Hettne et al., 2000a and b). Seen from this perspective, regionalism in its various guises is thus part and parcel of the "reorganisation of the state" and the emergence of new forms of governance in the context of globalisation.

The NRA calls for a transcendence of state-centrism and acknowledges the importance of market and society actors in regionalism. Through its origins in critical IPE the NRA is particularly focused on who are the driving actors of region-building, what interests, motives, ideas and identities shape and drive regionalisation, as well as who are the winners and losers in these processes. It is here argued that this perspective is highly relevant for the study of modes of governance and identifying the dominant distributions of power within these structures (see Söderbaum, 2002).

Why governance? Somewhat ironically, even among "globalists" there is increasing agreement that some "regulation" and "governance" is needed in the contemporary global political economy. Such a "return of governance" is dependent on the possibility of conceiving a new social and political space other than classical notions of Westphalia, and also new transnational actors for, and behind, the implementation of new modes of governance. Differently expressed, the current interest in governance reflects the decline or reorientation of (state) government in the context of globalisation. Seen from this perspective, the emergence of governance is a consequence of the unbundling of state functions, including government but also encompassing all new forms of 'systems of rules in which goals are pursued through the exercise of control' (Rosenau, 1997: 145). In much of the debate on governance, the concept has been used in a rather loose, normative way, often as "global governance" or "good governance". I believe that the concept of governance should be freed from solely thinking in such positive terms and rather used in all those situations in which the general definition applies, whether we favour these situations or not.

National government can be negative (or "bad") and so can governance, although governance must not be confused with government (although it also encompasses the latter). In order to understand the modes of governance emerging in the new world order and whose interests they serve, it should be recognised that they are more than simply formal-public systems of rule and authority structures for goal achievement. Needless to say, states often remain important role-players, but non-state actors are also involved in the construction and implementation of governance for different purposes, not only in the public interest. Furthermore, the prevailing view that authority and governance simply "disappears" or is weakened hand in hand with weakened, "failed" or collapsed states in Africa should be challenged. The deterioration of government does not necessarily imply the deterioration of governance, and as this chapter shows, authority and governance can take more informal and disguised forms. Governance is constructed by certain actors and for certain purposes, and our task is to assess them.

The analysis is structured as follows. The next two sections are mainly descriptive and can be seen as necessary point of departures. The first seeks to provide an overview of the institutional and organisational landscape that surrounds the MDC, while the second sketches the particular planning and implementation processes of the MDC. The third (and main) section of the chapter makes a critical assessment of governance in the MDC. This analysis addresses some of the key aspects of governance in the MDC: political champions; the non-bureaucratic and "networked" institutional structure; the fast-tracking of design and implementation; national and provincial relations; and finally local participation. In the conclusion the threads are brought together and the lessons to be learnt for future SDIs in southern Africa are dwelt upon.

The Institutional Landscape Surrounding the MDC

Although each SDI has to adjust to the different conditions under which it operates, there are some basic similarities and the officials at the Department of Trade and Industry (DTI) and the Development Bank of Southern Africa (DBSA) now speak of a generalised "SDI methodology" (see De Beer and Arkwright, chapter 2). According to this methodology, the institutional structure should be kept to a minimum, the main role of the institutions being to fast-track project implementation. This section seeks to map and identify the key institutions and agents in the institutional landscape surrounding the MDC.

The South African SDI programme is co-ordinated by the intersectoral and broadly-based Overall SDI Co-ordinating Committee (OSDICC). In the early stages OSDICC fed into a new inter-ministerial Cabinet Investment Cluster (CIC). The mandate of the CIC was to facilitate national and provincial co-ordination of investment promotion (i.e. bridge the gap between the national and provincial development programmes). The CIC was a powerful forum that reported directly to the Cabinet and proved important when rapid decisions needed to be made in order to facilitate large new investments. The OSDICC's meetings are attended by all SDI project managers as well as a broad range of senior representatives of national government departments and parastatals involved in the SDI process. It includes representatives of most government departments, parastatal finance and investment agencies, including the Development Bank of Southern Africa (DBSA), Investment South Africa and the Industrial Development Corporation (IDC), Transnet, Portnet and Spoornet, the Council for Scientific and Industrial Research (CSIR) and the Agricultural Research Council. The parastatal development finance agencies have been active participants from the start of the programme. This is particularly so in the case of the DBSA which at an early stage seconded staff and offices to project managers and provided legal support in terms of contracting and auditing etc. The IDC has been engaged in identifying "bankable" investment projects, while CSIR has re-oriented some of its activities to support the programme (see Hall, 1998).

Initially OSDICC used to meet every three weeks, which however became difficult to maintain because of the logistics of all the participants getting to a single location so frequently. The number of participants increased hand in hand with new SDIs. For these and other reasons the OSDICC was then split into two entities: firstly, the Co-ordination Committee of the so-called resource–based SDIs, and secondly, the Regional SDI Committee (RESDIC), to which the MDC belongs. These two committees meet much more infrequently and, according to Arkwright, 'most of us miss the regularity of the OSDICC process'.[1]

Another change of the institutional landscape during 2000 was that the Special Projects Directorate of the DTI was demobilised and instead the co-ordination of the SDI programme was supported and pushed by the DBSA. As mentioned above, the DBSA has always been directly involved in the SDI programme and its involvement has increased, which has been regarded as necessary to move away from bureaucracy and to enable the SDI programme to have a measure of independence from direct public policy.

One novel feature of the SDI methodology is that each SDI has (at least) two so called political champions—two high-ranking elected politicians at the national and provincial level—who can ensure political commitment and practical support for the process internationally (see De Beer and Arkwright, chapter 2). In the case of the MDC there has in effect been a large number of high-ranking political champions involved.

The project manager is the person chiefly responsible for implementing the SDI. In international SDIs, such as the MDC, there should be a project manager in each participating country. The South African MDC project manager (David Arkwright) is employed by and accountable to the DTI, while in Mozambique Francisca Soares works under the Ministry of Transport and Communications. According to the SDI methodology, it is the task of the project manager to put together a technical team, made up of officials from government and parastatals as well as consultants and other relevant experts. These should then provide the expertise needed to "drive" the MDC process during the initial stages. These project and task teams should be dissolved when their work has been completed (see next section).

On the provincial level there is (was) an intersectoral Maputo Development Corridor Provincial Technical Committee (PTC) (Mitchell, 1998: 760). The PTC is chaired by the Chief Director of Economic Affairs in Mpumalanga, who is the officer responsible for the MDC provincial processes. The committee is to co-ordinate the activities of different parts of the provincial administration, and it looks at environmental/strategic issues, agriculture, roads and transport, local government, tourism and small, micro and medium scale enterprises (SMMEs). The PTC consists of representatives of most departments in provincial government but also several representatives of national government—as well as from Limpopo Province—also participate in the PTC. There have been various sources of financial and technical assistance, creating resources for a number of specialised committees and teams. For instance, the World Bank has been supportive of the Strategic Environmental Management Plan (SEMP) in Mpumalanga. A provincial support programme for the MDC was also developed, which included a number of important studies on environment, SMMEs and sector planning studies in agriculture and tourism.

At later stages the Mpumalanga Investment Initiative (MII) has become a key driver in contributing to investment implementation in the Mpumalanga province. The MII is a one-stop investment agency, focused on investment promotion and assistance to potential investors. It offers services such as market information; facilitation with feasibility studies; assistance with application of incentives; relocation assistance; facilitation of finance; assistance with work permits; assistance in obtaining factory space/land; joint venture facilitation; fast-tracking of applications; and assistance with exports from Mpumalanga.

Implementation and institutional development has been lagging behind in Mozambique, and decision-making has remained centralised to the President and a few ministries/ministers, particularly the Ministry of Transport and Communications, the Department of Public Works and the Road Authority. Through the Bureau for the Co-ordination of Development Corridors (GPZ), Mozambique has a somewhat similar structure as that in South Africa. The GPZ is an umbrella bureau with one technical unit for every development/transport corridor in Mozambique, i.e. Maputo, Limpopo, Lubombo, Beira, Nacala and Zambezi Valley. That is, it seems that after a slow start Mozambique has decided to pursue their corridor programme with substantial enthusiasm. The Investment Promotion Centre of Mozambique (CPI) has also been involved in the process and it performs similar duties as the MII in Mpumalanga and Investment South Africa.

Finally, in the original plan the Maputo Corridor Company (MCC) was supposed to manifest the institutionalisation of the MDC, be the legal entity at the local/provincial level and bring together local and business actors, provide support, information monitoring and contribute to capacity-building (De Beer and Arkwright, chapter 2). The establishment of the MCC has been delayed due to a lack of capacity and commitment at both local and provincial level, both amongst public and private actors, particularly in Mozambique but also in Mpumalanga.

Planning and Implementation Phases of the MDC

The special planning and implementation procedures are essential components of the SDI methodology, which have been developed in order to reflect the transnational character, the (extremely) short time-frame and the project-driven approach of the initiatives. This planning process emphasises speedy implementation and the removal of bottlenecks and constraints to investment, which are often infrastructural in nature (roads, ports, railways) or trade-related (border posts, trade procedures). The initial phases should be driven by a loose and fluid network consisting of the political champions, central government institutions, the different line departments (mainly transport, and trade and industry), the project managers and the technical teams. Then, in the last stage of implementation, in the so-called "exit phase", the administration should be decentralised to the provincial and local institutions, particularly their investment promotion agencies, whose main brief is to facilitate new investment in the region. There is considerable emphasis on "fast-tracking" project implementation, and the set-up, appraisal, packaging and launch of a SDI at the investors conference is supposed to be completed within 12-18 months. The exit strategy is given longer time, up to two years.

More specifically, the first thing performed in the setting up of a SDI is to appoint a project manager. The project manager organises an initial conceptual workshop and identifies promising sectors for investment, the main bottlenecks for development and the main investment opportunities in the area. The manager also sets up a technical team and a project identification team, made up of officials from government and parastatals as well as consultants and other relevant experts. Yet another main task of the project manager is to identify local "champions" and stakeholders to provide the programme with legitimacy, and to ensure that there is an organisation that can secure implementation upon the decentralisation of functions to provincial and local authorities (Jourdan, 1998; Hall, 1998).

After the set-up and pre-feasibility phase and the establishment of institutional structures, with political and technical teams etc., the process moves into the identification and "packaging" of investment opportunities. Ideas for investment projects are widely solicited, including from local and provincial stakeholders. The main criterion for projects is that they must be "bankable", that is, they must offer a commercially viable return on investment (Jourdan, 1998). The DBSA and the IDC play a significant role in identifying and testing the feasibility of projects. The next task is to match potential domestic and international investors with investment opportunities and to raise the profile of the area as an international investment destination, typically through an investors' conference. After the MDC investors' conference (held in May 1996), the technical team and project identification teams were dissolved, and the MDC was supposed to be "handed over" through the so-called "exit strategy" to the provincial and local institutional structure. The provincial and local institutional structure should then continue to identify investment projects and match them with potential investors.

Implementation Phases of the MDC

PHASE	ACTIVITY
1. Set Up Phase	Appointment of project manager; gathering of socio-economic and institutional data on the loosely defined corridor area.
2. Pre-Feasibility	Pre-feasibility appraisal of data; organisation of conceptual workshop, development framework and spatial definition (led by project manager).
3. Institutional	Establishment of structures at the political, official and technical capacity levels, e.g. set-up of political team; interdepartmental team; technical team; working groups; identification of local champions.
4. Feasibility	Together with key stakeholders, further development of the conceptual framework into a terms of reference for more detailed appraisal. Identification and appraisal of lead projects and the developmental programme of action. DBSA and IDC play significant role in identifying and testing projects.
5. Packaging	Finalisation of a detailed development perspective document, which indicates a list of viable projects and investment opportunities.
6. Launch	Launching of the MDC, at the investors conference, to present vision, objectives, perspective, anchor projects and investment opportunities; establishment of investment promotion mechanism and implementation capacity. Technical teams and project identification teams are dissolved.
7. Exit Strategy	Institutional arrangements to facilitate momentum and implementation of the initiative and the 'hand over' to provincial structure, e.g. the establishment of the Maputo Corridor Company and the consolidation of Provincial Investment Promotion Agencies. Establishment of clusters for selected sectors in the MDC area, which bring firms across the supply chain together and enhance their collective efficiencies.

Governing the Corridor

This section seeks to make an inventory and assessment of the governance structures in the MDC, with a particular focus on who decides what, with what means and what are the patterns of exclusion and inclusion. The analysis highlights the following aspects of governance: (i) political champions; (ii) the network structure; (iii) the fast-tracking of design and implementation; (iv) national and provincial relations; and finally (v) local participation.

Political Champions

The implementation of a SDI requires considerable political commitment and political will at relevant levels of government (see De Beer and Arkwright, chapter 2). The political commitment provided by the political champions is supposed to increase co-ordination and integration between all the government departments that are involved in the process. It appears to be difficult to mobilise a higher degree of political commitment to a development project than what has been ensured in the case of the MDC. The project has received political commitment not only from the very highest levels, in the form of the presidents of the two countries but also from a number of highly-ranked politicians, such as the Ministers of Transport in both countries, the Minister of Trade and Industry in South Africa, as well as the (former) Premier of Mpumalanga, Matthews Phosa. In addition some influential ANC policy-makers, such as Ketso Gordhan (Director General at the Department of Transport, DOT) and Paul Jourdan (Deputy Director General at the DTI), have pushed the project. There is little doubt that this political commitment initially contributed to effective decision-making and speedily implementation of the MDC.

The strategy with political champions is particularly interesting in view of the more or less chronic difficulties ensuring implementation of most types of intergovernmental regional co-operation projects in Africa in the past. It appears that the high level of political commitment can be explained by the fact that the MDC has been a test case of the SDI programme. In fact, it is suggested that any failure of the MDC would possibly have undermined the whole SDI programme in both countries, thus the MDC simply "had to work", and it was imperative to mobilise whatever political support was needed in order to overcome the hurdles along the way. In Mozambique the MDC in general and the Mozal project in particular served as the show-case for proving that industrial projects could be both implemented and be on time. Seen from this perspective, it was more important that the Mozal was completed on time, rather than ensuring that it had a democratic input or that it involved Mozambican contractors and labour to any large extent.

Exactly how important the high level of political commitment has been for implementation is difficult to estimate. That it has been important is illustrated by the fact that, as an anonymous official stated: 'at one stage the whole project was rapidly approaching crisis, which served as a major wake-up call for Mozambique, and a new more senior minister took over the Department of Transport...[This] led to the MDC receiving a boom overnight and [it] was then almost driven by Mozambique'.

The crucial importance of political commitment is also illustrated by what happened as a result of the new Premier in Mpumalanga, who succeeded Matthews Phosa. While Phosa was very committed to the MDC, the new Premier, Ndaweni Mahlungu, has clearly had other priorities than the MDC and projects associated with the legacy of Phosa (De Beer and Arkwright, chapter 2; Ngwenya and Taylor, chapter 6). One anonymous official confirms that 'everything has changed because it was all linked to Phosa'. In fact, as a provincial policy-maker points out, 'the Corridor has collapsed as a provincial thing...the Committee [i.e. the PTC] is officially restructured but basically the province has walked away from the process'.[2] According to the South African project manager, the 'SDI programme no longer has the requisite political support to enable it to keep going as we know it'.[3] After the collapse of the provincial committee, the Mpumalanga Investment Initiative (MII) has become the only provincial institution involved in the MDC process. This shows that the institutional structure is weak as well as heavily dependent on what particular individuals happen to be the political champions, thereby adding a striking amount of uncertainty and instability to the project.

Network Structure

The institutional structure of the MDC is "networked" and non-bureaucratic, with a more or less minimalist approach to institutions. The network structure is designed in order to meet the challenge of interdepartmental co-ordination and to maintain flexibility and speed in planning and implementation. Although this structure consists of numerous new committees, sub-committees, project and technical teams, it builds mainly on existing institutional capacities and draws together capacities and policy-makers in a loosely organised and flexible network structure.

According to its architects, one strength of this approach is that it has sustained interdepartmental co-operation, and that 'it is slowly teaching government departments to work together' (Ismail and Jourdan, 1998). However, even if it mainly seeks to build on existing institutional resources, progress depends on the quality and strength of these capacities. Such strategy is risky when skills and capacities do not exist or are weak, which is the reality not only in Mpumalanga and in Maputo, but also in several quarters in Gauteng. To some extent the lack of institutional capacities has been catered for, as illustrated by the creation of a new PPP-unit in the Department of Finance and new units in the DBSA as well as the IDC. But this has mainly been done at the central government level. Ismail and Jourdan are correct in that: '[t]his ad hoc institution building has happened as we've gone along, on a crisis management basis so far. This has to be more packaged than before' (Ismail and Jourdan, 1998).

Although there are a number of different committees and actors involved in the MDC process, there is a general lack of formal institutions and bureaucratic frameworks on both sides of the border (although this is/was particularly deep on the Mozambican side). Many committees and task teams are only temporary in nature. This has resulted in the situation where except for the project manager there is no organisational and legal structure that represents and takes responsibility for the MDC. It is difficult to track the centre of decision-making and power as well as to understand where responsibility and accountability lies. The DTI is obviously a main player but it does not seek responsibility since it wants to "hand over" the initiative to the province, whereas the province on its side has not been part of the design and build up of the MDC and feels it does not "own" the initiative. As the South African project manager points out, 'it needs to be established who is carrying the Corridor'.[4]

Considering the size of the SDI projects, they are weakly institutionalised. There is an intention to be non-institutionalised and non-bureaucratic in order to be flexible and adjustable to private and contextual demands. However, this simply implies a loss of public participation and democratic control in the decision-making and implementation process. Again, informality serves the interests of the powerful and wealthy, especially a small ruling political elite and transnational capitalist interests. More serious drawbacks are that the network structure creates a rather diffuse power and responsibility structure without a clear centre of decision-making, and it is not particularly suited to carry out conventional bureaucratic procedures.

The minimalist and informal institutional structure has led to the situation where the MDC strategy depends heavily on the use of informal power and "political capital" in order to ensure progress. However, 'the bureaucratic dangers inherent in this approach are obvious; a guiding SDI policy statement notes "that there is always a risk of allowing certain key role players, including government departments, to get left behind in the process, thereby creating the impression of exclusivity"...' (Hall, 1998, fn. 12). Differently expressed, the informal network structure is mainly designed and effective for those on the "inside" rather than those "outside" the network. As will be elaborated below, the provinces and the citizenry in particular are on the "outside".

Fast-tracking... or Slow-tracking?

A quick planning and implementation process is central to the whole idea of the MDC and the SDI process more generally. The MDC management team is supposed to identify obstacles to investments and implementation and then speedily mobilise political support from the political champions in order to generate momentum and facilitate "delivery". Key architects of the MDC have characterised such fast-tracking 'like rowing a canoe with holes—if you stop you sink' (Ismail and Jourdan, 1998). There are some strengths with this strategy. Through its speed and the close link between input/effort and output/delivery, it provides a strategy for implementation and gives concrete meaning to the process of cross-border co-operation in a way which many other comprehensive projects have failed to do in the past. 'The main strength of the SDI methodology', according to the South

African project manager, 'is that it has brought a new approach, through a precise set of steps, which could get things moving'.[5] The Mozambican project manager has argued that another strength is that 'it started to challenge things...and brought new things to Mozambique...back in 1995 it seemed that such push-approach was actually needed'.[6]

Nevertheless, in certain respects the speed was *too fast* for Mozambique, as well as for South Africa, especially with regard to the inclusion of non-governmental actors and the citizenry.[7] According to a key role-player in the process, 'the extreme emphasis on speed has been counter-productive', and, 'the fast-track approach is slower than a slow-track approach'.[8] This is because design and implementation must be so quick that there exists no time for rational bureaucratic decision-making that is adjusted to local conditions and sensitive to the interests of concerned actors and institutions. The extremely rapid design and decision-making process is particularly problematic in a context with low institutional capacities, such as the one in Mpumalanga and Mozambique. Several key officials involved in the MDC project emphasised the need for the development of institutions and management systems that can ensure a more coherent and well-thought-through policy and decision-making process (see De Beer and Arkwright, chapter 2).

The fast-track approach is risky also for the quality of capital investments by the private and public sectors. To offset these risks, the government has mobilised considerable technical expertise from both the public and private sectors to back-up the process, mainly in the form of consultancy and expert teams. Although such expert teams are important, the proclaimed "urgency" has not allowed any time for discussing the *content* of the MDC project and letting all parties understand what the MDC actually is and is not about (Söderbaum and Taylor, chapter 4). Essentially the MDC has been designed at the drawing tables in Gauteng and quickly enforced in a top-down manner, without ensuring that provincial and local actors are integrated and consulted or that it can work for the people living in the corridor area.

National and Provincial Relations

A network consisting of various national institutions has been the driving force of the first main phase of the MDC. The MDC was then supposed to be "handed over" to provincial and local institutions during the "exit phase". The problem is that the central government and its development finance institutions have neither been enthusiastic nor successful in integrating and involving provincial and local governments and institutions in policy and decision-making. Here it should be noted that there is a fundamental difference between the way the DOT and the DTI handle relationships with the provinces. According to a provincial economist participating in the PTC, 'initially the Department of Transport took an enlightened stance and understood that the Province needed support ... it actively sought to provide impetus to the province, but when the SDI Unit at the DTI took over the process was centralised [because] the DTI works under the assumption that the province cannot do anything.'[9]

One set of problems with design and decision-making of the MDC is related to the investors' conference. In the SDI approach much effort is placed on the design and packaging of investment projects to be presented at the investors' conference. Provincial and local actors are not integrated into identification and design of these projects, which in turn has created a host of different problems. The CEO of the MII claims that 'it is embarrassing to market and present the projects inherited from the investors' conference. The investors' conference was more like a wishing list...the MII does not know the details of these projects...and the projects were not adjusted to local conditions. [There was] bad sequencing of the MDC approach...and even if the MII was not created at such early stage...the MII ought to have been involved much earlier in the process'.[10] As a consequence of this exclusion and problems, the MII concentrated on the cluster processes and downstream production instead of the projects stemming from the investors' conference.

The national-provincial relationship has thus proved to be a flaw in the design and implementation of the MDC. Central government institutions have pushed the project, but due to capacity constraints on the provincial and local level the assumed "urgency" has left these actors outside of any real design and implementation. There is a poor (and sometimes even non-existent) relationship between central government/institutions and provincial institutions. In a strong critique of the SDI methodology, Hall suggests that central government institutions, including the national conglomerates, Portnet and the IDC, must operate better at the provincial level. 'The challenge for the SDI Office in the DTI is to convince these agencies to provide the correct incentives for changes in the relationships of key local organisations and actors' (Hall, 1998: 14). This argument is similar to Lewis and Bloch (1998: 753), who claim that 'cluster initiatives and other industrial support programmes to enhance competitiveness need to develop a clearer regional/provincial focus, and that the SDIs need to design their mechanisms with a greater emphasis on strengthening regional [i.e. provincial] agglomerations and clusters' (also see Amin, 1998).

By way of summing up, the mode of governance in the MDC is centred on the assumption that in order to maintain fast-track delivery, the province or locally constituted public "partners" can be by-passed or side-stepped if they are deemed "unfit" for one reason or another, such as being "too political", lacking capacity, competence, vision and commitment etc. According to Bernstein (1999), 'this marked one clear limit of SDIs, namely that they can contribute to institutional capacity (e.g. inter-departmental liaison and co-ordination, local planning and management capacity, human resource development) when initial conditions are relatively favourable, but not when local development requires more gradual/evolutionary and more "political" (participatory) processes of institution building'. In effect such by-passing means that the proposed decentralisation strategy is reversed: 'the MDC is actually centralised rather than decentralised'.[11]

Local Participation

There has been very limited communication between central government actors and local governments, local communities and local private sector. 'It is a paradox that, although the Corridor is well-known nationally and internationally, many local communities which will be directly affected by the development have very little information about the project' (Mitchell, 1998: 760). The official view from the SDI Unit within the DTI is that there is some degree of "participation" and that the SDIs are supposed to deal with locals to some extent, but that 'it is not a deep-rooted participatory process' (Ismail and Jourdan, 1998). Local participation is supposed to come in only through the exit phase. The problem is that this eliminates stakeholders from the basic design and prioritisation of projects. Furthermore, this does not travel well with the official rhetoric that the MDC is supposed to foster participatory development. The MDC project is reasonably "inclusive" and open for big business and central government institutions and (capable and resource-rich) actors in the national departments, the DBSA, the IDC, Investment South Africa, the CSIR and so forth, but it is exclusionary in regard to weaker actors and people outside this inner core of the network. The purpose of this closed and largely undemocratic network is to implement gigantic investment projects and to deal with a few dozen "big" investors rather than large groups of dispossessed people at the local level.

It appears that rather than a genuine public governance mechanism, what is emerging is a partnership between the political elite and global capital supported by the IFIs and the donor community. This semi-private form of governance employs the rhetoric of people-centred development but in reality the main concern is, effectively, jobless growth, foreign exchange earnings and little else. The role of public governance is reduced to boosting new bankable and commercially viable investment projects, often of gigantic proportions such as with the case of the Mozal aluminium smelter in Matola outside Maputo (Söderbaum and Taylor, chapter 4; Hentz, chapter 7).

In this context it should be mentioned that the investors' conference was intended to create opportunities for small- and medium-size businesses, in the way that local businesses are encouraged to network and form joint ventures with foreign and non-local investors. This has not worked satisfactorily, however, and it is appears that in its current design the MDC is not well suited for the inclusion of the local market demands and the social forces.

Most evidence suggests that local participation is equally badly served by the provincial government (Söderbaum and Taylor, chapter 4; Ngwenya and Taylor, chapter 6). Some policy-makers recognise that the lack of local participation constitutes a serious deficiency of the MDC. In order to meet this challenge the Mpumalanga provincial government tried to develop a comprehensive communication strategy, together with an innovative community tracking system. Unfortunately, this suddenly ended with changes in the provincial leadership in Mpumalanga. The question of local participation is not just about democratic instinct however, it also means that problems are created which sooner or later have to be dealt with, once again illustrating a situation where the fast-track in effect becomes a slow-track.

Under present circumstances there is no convincing evidence that neither the state nor the provincial government will be able to build participatory and people-centred governance mechanisms in the MDC. As indicated above, the role of the governance structures are simply to facilitate private and commercially viable investment projects and not much else. For instance, then Deputy Director General responsible for the SDI process at the DTI asserts that the strategy 'is too important...to be derailed by vested interests' (*Mail and Guardian*, Johannesburg, 7 November 1997). This shows for whom and for what purpose the governance mechanisms are erected.

It must be recognised that there have been many types of local protests against the MDC. These appear to be the result of the way the MDC projects have been designed and implemented from the beginning. Perhaps the most contentious issue of local participation concerns "ownership" and for whom the corridor is actually constructed. This issue is particularly heated in the case of the N4 toll road and the Mozal project (Ngwenya and Taylor, chapter 6; Hentz, chapter 7). In both these projects there have been very limited consultation with local communities over important issues and dialogue is only really enacted when effected local inhabitants complain. The fact of the matter is that the MDC is not designed to involve bottom-up forces and facilitate local participation. This in turn questions the ownership of the micro-region and gives it a "democratic deficit". These problems must not be ignored, but may actually undermine the role of the state. Similarly to several other African countries and somewhat ironically resembling the apartheid state, which was an instrument in the hands of the Whites, the new (neo-liberal) state may be looked upon as an "external" agent, implementing top-down projects in alliance with international investors rather than its own citizenry (see Söderbaum and Taylor, chapter 4).

Conclusion: Lessons for Development Corridors and SDIs in Southern Africa

The MDC is the most high profile of the SDIs in southern Africa, and in official rhetoric it is claimed to be a major success. There is little doubt that micro-regions and SDIs will increase in number and scope in southern Africa. Some SDIs and development corridors have been or are in the process of being implemented, while others are merely potential and may not necessarily be implemented. A host of different countries, institutions and actors are promoting the construction of SDIs and development corridors in southern Africa. For instance, the South African government has offered to aid regional SDIs throughout the SADC region by transferring the lessons learned and the skills gained during the execution of the SDIs in South Africa. In fact, President Thabo Mbeki has stated that the SDIs in southern Africa form part of the vision of the "African Renaissance" (DBSA, 2001b). Likewise, the mandate of the DBSA has recently been extended to cover the whole SADC region, and this institution is now involved in several of the regional SDIs. Other important South African institutions, such as the IDC and the CSIR, are also participating in the overall regional SDI processes.

With this said, however, South Africa's engagement in the region and in promoting such SDIs is very contentious. If the regional SDIs, when implemented, are 'entirely geared towards the needs of South African companies...the support for this type of regional project would possibly evaporate relatively quickly' (Dieter et al., 2001). Here it should be noted that there is an indication that South Africa is backing off, possibly in favour of individual country programmes or a more multilateral/regional approach (if so probably within the framework of SADC). Only time can tell whether such an approach actually will take off (see Tevera and Chimhowu, chapter 3). In fact, SADC has declared that SDIs, transport and development corridors have 'always' been the 'SADC's way of doing things'.[12] However, SADC's actual involvement in the MDC has been rather muted and has not impacted to any degree, at least not in South Africa. It appears that the MDC's management has been deliberately kept at a bilateral level because of the differences in opinion regarding the notion of private investment projects and PPPs and towards SADC as an organisation.

Drawing lessons from the MDC for future development corridors and SDIs in southern Africa is necessarily somewhat speculative, but still a fruitful exercise. It is quite clear that the political champions have proved to be important players in the MDC project, and there are strong reasons to believe that they should also be key components in any type of regional SDI. Considering the centralised decision-making structure in most SADC countries, it appears that the political champions must be in the highest centres of decision-making, preferably a key minister or even the President. As revealed by the crisis occurring as a result from the change of premier in Mpumalanga, a weak champion may in fact sabotage the whole process.

There are certain strengths with the network structure. First, it can ensure a quick and flexible planning and decision-making process. Second, this structure draws together capacities and policy-makers in a loosely organised and flexible network, which innovatively enhances interdepartmental co-ordination and so-called co-operative government. Third, the network structure is particularly interesting in light of the fact that while conventional state-driven regional ventures have proved to be rather cumbersome and rigid, the MDC as a governance mechanism involves a more limited number of partners and is more flexible, thus offering greater scope for experimentation and speed in changing operations.

Having said this, it must be more deeply assessed whether the fluid and loosely organised network structure is suitable for the existing bureaucratic and institutional realities in the neighbouring countries. Patterns of decision-making about major resources may often be centralised, which may lead to problems with practical implementation within a network structure. By the same token, the interdepartmental co-ordination and co-operation in the South African SDI programme may not be working in some of the other SADC countries, where the highest level of government is often needed to get things going (DTI, 1998a).

Furthermore, the network structure requires that institutions and capacities are strong, capable and competent, which was not the case in Mpumalanga and Mozambique (and to some extent neither on the central national level in South Africa). As a result, actors in these locations experienced serious difficulties. Due to the fact that the institutional capacities in many neighbouring countries are weaker than in South Africa (including Mpumalanga), the viability of the network structure has to be more carefully analysed. In the process of building regional SDIs it seems that there must be a stronger focus on both formal and informal institutional capacity building than has been the case in the MDC. A closely related proposition is to create a more structured "organisation" that takes responsibility for the process, provides a legal and regulatory framework and becomes a recognised "driver".

In view of the fact that many large-scale projects tend to stagnate, fast-tracking is positive in the sense that it maintains momentum and provides stakeholders with a link between input and output. However, the institutional limitations and political realities in the SADC countries suggest that it may be difficult to sustain the high speed emphasised in the SDI methodology. Instead of a multiplier effect and a kick-start, a fast-tracked SDI faces the risk of being yet another project with no or few local links and thus disentangled from the realities on the ground. As suggested by the MDC, the high speed may also have negative repercussions on rational decision-making as well as the quality of investment.

The national-provincial relation constitutes a weak link in the MDC. The co-operation started out quite well, but gradually the MDC project was centralised rather than decentralised. As suggested by the case of the MDC a top-down and centralised strategy can work on the central government level, but it tends to be ineffective on the ground as well as being met with local resistance. The handing over and exit strategy did not work satisfactorily in the case of the MDC, a fact that needs to be accommodated and rethought in any future regional SDIs. Clearly, there needs to be a sound balance between centralised and decentralised policy-making, which allows a certain degree of provincial and local participation at earlier stages in the process. This would also imply making institution- and capacity-building as an integral part of the SDI from the outset. However, and this needs to be emphasised, unless there is commitment and resources for empowering the provinces and the people living in the particular SDI area, one radical alternative can be to "keep" the SDI as a top-down and centralistic programme. This means not advancing the false illusion that the provincial and local actors suddenly will have the capacity and commitment to carry out a programme that they only have been involved in at the very last stages of implementation. Although the MDC is surrounded by the rhetoric of people-centred development, in reality the main concern is infrastructural development through PPPs and the encouragement of private "mega-projects". In effect this public governance mechanism is simply to boost new bankable and commercially viable investment projects, often of gigantic proportions, rather than ensure local participation in design, policy-making and implementation. In this sense, an open acknowledgement about the nature of top-down SDIs and their limited ability for local empowerment and transformation might be a more honest approach, rather than dressing such projects up as "people-centred" and "holistic".

Notes

1. Personal communication, David Arkwright, South African Project Manager of MDC, Nelspruit, 27 November 2000.
2. Interview with Jonathan Mitchell, Special Projects and Policy Unit, Mpumalanga Province, Nelspruit, 5 April 2000
3. Interview with David Arkwright, South African Project Manager of MDC, Nelspruit, 27 November 2000.
4. Interview with David Arkwright, South African Project Manager of MDC, Nelspruit, 12 April 2000.
5. Interview with David Arkwright, South African Project Manager of MDC, Nelspruit, 16 March 1999.
6. Interview with Francisca Henriqueta Soares, MDC Project Manager, Mozambican Ministry of Transport and Communications, Maputo, 10 April 2000.
7. Interview with Francisca Henriqueta Soares, MDC Project Manager, Mozambican Ministry of Transport and Communications, Maputo, 10 April 2000.
8. Interview with Jonathan Mitchell, Special Projects and Policy Unit, Mpumalanga Provincial Government, Nelspruit, South Africa, 5 April 2000.
9. Interview with Jonathan Mitchell, Special Projects and Policy Unit, Mpumalanga Provincial Government, Nelspruit, South Africa, 5 April 2000.
10. Interview with Gordon Griffiths, Chief Executive Officer, Mpumalanga Investment Initiative, Nelspruit, 4 April 2000.
11. Interview with Jonathan Mitchell, Special Projects and Policy Unit, Mpumalanga Provincial Government, Nelspruit, South Africa, 5 April 2000.
12. Interview with Dr. Alfredo Namitete, Chairman, Committee of Senior Officials, Southern African Transport and Communications Commission (SATCC), Maputo, 6 April 2000.

Chapter 6

Public-Private Partnerships and African Development: The Case of the N4 Toll Road

Xenia Ngwenya and Ian Taylor

In the current era where neo-liberalism remains hegemonic as the guiding ideology for economic (and by extension, political) projects, there has been a qualitative shift from using the state as the prime engine of development. This has occurred at both the state and supra-state level. This chapter examines the way in which the new thinking on the role of the private sector in development has been taken on board within the MDC. It particularly focuses on the public-private partnership (PPP) schemes that stake out much of the MDC, with a focus on the N4 toll road. At the same time, this chapter examines the way in which PPPs have been adopted by African multilateral bodies as the preferred "solution" to Africa's developmental impasse. One of the multilateral institutions that has embraced this development paradigm and has become a strong proponent thereof is the United Nations Economic Commission for Africa (ECA). The change in developmental philosophy by the ECA reflects, in part, the wish by the current Secretary-General of the United Nations (UN), Kofi Annan, to intensify the involvement of the private sector in the activities of the UN and its agencies. While this involvement of non-state actors is not completely new, the current increase in emphasis and intensification of the UN's programme to encourage the private sector as an (if not *the*) engine for development mirrors the primacy given to the non-public sector in the MDC. In this sense, the role of private enterprise in the MDC fits with the agenda of the ECA and the UN and perhaps may be seen as a pilot project for the effectiveness, if not the credibility, of PPPs as a means to promote development in Africa in the new millennium.

Public-Private Partnerships

The emergence of the PPP approach in providing the supply and/or renovation of infrastructural projects in itself reflects the hegemony of neo-liberalism in the current era. With its emphasis on low public expenditure and a concentration on trade deficit reduction and low national debt, the call to increasingly involve the private sector in supplying services formerly provided by the state has become almost universalised. In this sense, the PPP philosophy inherent in the SDI project(s) is reflective of international trends. Indeed, over the last few years in Europe, for instance, the use of PPPs has gained momentum and a number of transport infrastructural schemes have been pursued. Examples that may be cited include the M1/M15 Motorway and M5 Motorway in Hungary; Warsaw Airport in Poland; and the Øresund Link between Sweden and Denmark. Furthermore, both the World Bank and the United Nations Development Programme (UNDP) advocate the usage of PPPs in providing or renovating services, as does the ECA (see below). The PPP philosophy then is not unique to SDIs and in fact draws upon past experience from other countries/regions.

The actual notion of a "PPP philosophy" may be a bit stretched as there are all manner of PPPs and no one particular definition. Indeed, PPPs can take on many varieties, whether it is the commercialisation of existing state activity to outright privatisation. Having said that, a working definition is possible. In general, PPPs may be said to be long-term contracts involving both the public and private sectors to supply and run infrastructure and/or services. This implies a sharing of responsibilities and a sharing of both the benefits and risk by the state and by the private sector. Essentially, 'PPPs represent indirect access by the government, through private partners, to resources provided by the private sector' (Leigland and Thomas, 1999: i).

This public-private involvement encompasses a whole variety of possible relationships between public and private actors for the supply of services. What can be said is that some degree of private participation in the delivery of traditionally state-provided services is essential. The "private sector" can be broadly defined to include any non-state actor(s). Thus, private enterprise, informal market actors, community-based organisations, non-governmental organisations (NGO), universities, and private individuals may all be included within the proviso of the "private" element within PPPs.

The attractiveness of PPPs within a structural framework where resources are limited and the availability of funding for large-scale infrastructural projects is severely constrained is self-evident. Unfortunately for the post-apartheid state, the damage wrought by forty years of National Party (mis)rule means that resources for infrastructural development (never mind renovation) are extremely limited. Such constraints are real and relate to the past, particularly as the National Party government increased the country's budget deficit from 0.9 per cent of GDP in 1989-90 to 10.8 per cent in 1993-94 through a reckless spending spree. Combined with a profligate policy towards the end of the National Party tenure to pump extra finances into civil servant pension funds, the stock of government debt rose roughly from R100 billion to R250 billion. It should be borne in mind that this increase in debt of R150 billion could have covered expenditure for essential services in South Africa for nearly twenty years (*Business Day*, Johannesburg, 15 September 1998). Criminally, in its *last year of power alone*, the National Party government increased the national debt by R60 billion (*Sunday Times*, Johannesburg, 15 May 1994). By doing so, the apartheid regime helped circumscribe any future room for government's manoeuvre. According to a recent report, by 1997 there was an accrued backlog for road infrastructure of R37 billion and that in 1997 alone, the shortfall for road infrastructure spending was R4.7 billion (*Mail and Guardian*, Johannesburg, 12-18 May 2000). Yet, road transport remains the dominant form of transport in Africa, underpinning any attempt to use trade as the engine of economic growth. Acknowledging this, the South African and Mozambican governments are in a major quandary in attempting to maintain an efficient and well-maintained road system, particularly within spatial areas designated as potential development corridors.

With the chronic fiscal constraints on financing road projects, the PPP approach then has an obvious attraction to the post-apartheid state if it means that an additional means to finance infrastructure and services is made available from sources other than the public purse. Indeed, the South African government has had a policy since 1997, via the National Roads Agency, of encouraging unsolicited bids from private companies as a means to increase the number of regional roads that are upgraded and tolled by the private sector. This policy was based on an understanding of the limits of the National Roads Agency's capacity and constraints, and was looking for avenues for PPPs to promote economic development by upgrading and/or constructing badly needed infrastructure. The unsolicited bid policy is a neat fit with the Department of Transport's own aim to downsize its involvement in developing transport infrastructure and promote PPPs. The policy relates only to the upgrading and development of toll roads and has a strong competitive tender element to it. The process is that a private sector company should submit a proposal to the National Roads Agency with details including a key plan, present traffic figures, a tolling strategy and minimum design standards and performance criteria. The Agency then considers the plan and, if it agrees, appoints the company as scheme developer to investigate the feasibility of the project. Once all involved parties are satisfied the scheme should go ahead, tender documents are compiled and a competitive tender process is undertaken to appoint a preferred bidder (*Business Day*, Johannesburg, 28 April 2000). It appears that the South African government is firmly committed to PPPs, with the establishment of a new PPP unit, announced in early 2000 (*Business Day*, Johannesburg , 24 February 2000).

The Economic Commission for Africa and PPPs

The processes outlined above fit with the suggestions made by the ECA regarding the importance of PPPs as engines of African development. In his foreword to the ECA's programme orientation, titled *The ECA and Africa: Accelerating a Continent's Development*, the General-Secretary of the ECA, Dr K.Y. Amoako, clearly states that the 'ECA's new approach is underpinned by the credo that effective, high-impact developmental work in Africa can only be achieved through concrete and sustained partnerships. With this in mind, we are keen to work with partners within the UN system as well as beyond it-in the private sector and civil society' (ECA, 1999: viii). The ECA is quite hopeful in its quest to strengthen its relationship with the private sector, taking as its cue pronouncements from bodies such as the World Bank that partnerships between different levels of government, the private sector, donor groups and civil society are essential requirements for effective development.

The ECA was established in 1958. It is one of the five regional commissions of the United Nations Economic and Social Council (ECOSOC), and is the regional arm of the UN in Africa. The original mandate of the ECA was to initiate, participate in and facilitate the economic development of Africa in order to raise the level of economic activity and standards of living; maintain and strengthen the economic relations between African countries and between Africa and the rest of the world; and to undertake or finance investigations into economic and technical problems of the continent (Department of Foreign Affairs, 2000a: 2). The ECA currently comprises fifty-three member states and as a sub-organ of the Economic and Social Council of the United Nations, it is financed from the UN's resources.

It is significant to note that prior to assuming his position as the Secretary-General of the ECA in 1995, Amoako worked for the World Bank—where much of the ideas regarding state-private sector-civil society partnerships gained prominence. Emphasis on "partnerships" as a major theme of the ECA gained prominence in 1996 when the ECA embarked on a reform and restructuring programme, based on the 'conviction that development assistance to Africa requires concerted effort and new forms of partnerships and collaboration among the stakeholders in the continent's development' (ECA, 1999: 2). It can be argued that Amoako—as the force behind the reforms—has propagated World Bank-style "partnerships". Indeed, in motivating the ECA's reform, one of the principles guiding the restructuring was that of 'establishing or retaining subsidiary bodies to enable the Commission to draw on the advice of experts from governments of member states but also the private sector and civil society groups in Africa' (ECA, 2000a: 6). The current programme orientation of the ECA was adopted in 1996 and is encapsulated under the title *Serving Africa Better: Strategic Directions for the Economic Commission for Africa* (ECA, 2000b), which identifies five categories of partners: African intergovernmental organisations; agencies of the UN system; African universities and research institutions; bilateral donors; and civil society groups (ECA, 2000b: 5). What is interesting to note about the partners identified is that when the document was drawn up, the private sector did not feature as an identified partner for the ECA. However, there has been a clear shift in thinking since then, with a move towards incorporating the private sector in "partnership" with the ECA.

The focus on partnerships by the ECA has been extended to the Sub-Regional Development Centres. In the Sub-Regional Development Centre for Southern Africa, for example, the theme of the Fifth Meeting of the Intergovernmental Committee of Experts in 1998 was "Building Effective Partnership". What was stressed at this gathering was the role of various partners in development in the region, including individuals, informal sector business, big business, civil society, and bilateral partners (Department of Foreign Affairs, 2000a: 9). As part of this Sub-Regional Development Centre, South Africa sought to identify areas in which it wished to engage its domestic partners with ECA. Of the issues that the ECA is currently focusing on, South Africa considers four to be of particular importance to itself, namely agriculture, population and social issues, industrial development and international trade (Department of Foreign Affairs, 2000b: 5). Even within these areas, the ECA considers the establishment of partnerships to be an essential means to achieving development. In 1999, for example. the ECA called on the help of the UN Industrial Development Organization (UNIDO), the OAU and the African Development Bank to organise a conference on "Industrial Partnerships and Investment in Africa".

What makes the ECA approach somewhat interesting is that while it embraces a concept which is considered to be a product of the current neo-liberal world order, it simultaneously claims an approach that will be uniquely "African" and suited to the needs of the many underdeveloped nations of Africa. One could be selective in one's view of how this proposal—what Amoako calls an "Africa-led" approach—will work. It could be viewed as an effort not to be seen as blind advocates of the ideologies of those international actors with more powerful voices, or alternatively as an acknowledgement that the current system can work for Africa if Africa is given the stage to cast her own play. Having said that, the ECA's recommendations for PPPs are mirrored in the ongoing processes along the MDC. Whilst there is no evidence that the projects within the MDC, particularly the PPPs, spring from ECA positions, it is interesting that the main developmental programme being advanced by Pretoria to promote regional interaction shares a number of similar positions as those supported by the ECA; thereby being an example of "policy fit". The actual components of one such PPP in the MDC—the N4 toll road—is what we turn to next.

The N4 Toll Road

The importance of the N4 toll road is crucial, for the success of the N4 toll road (or otherwise) will be a sign as regards the feasibility of PPPs in financing southern Africa's infrastructure needs. According to one Mozambican source, transport infrastructure is vital as it creates an enabling environment through which everything else can follow.[1] The toll road is 440km long and extends from Witbank to Maputo. The overall project involves the (selective) rehabilitation and upgrading of an existing 390km route from Balmoral (20km west of Witbank) to Moamba, and the construction of a new 50km-long route from Moamba to Maputo. The last 90km piece of the road, all situated in Mozambique, is estimated to be a third of the overall cost (*Business Report*, Johannesburg, 22 June 1999).

The new route, cutting 150km off the trip between Gauteng and Maputo, and shortening travelling time to around four hours, is the most extensive infrastructure project in the MDC. The concession for the toll road was awarded after an open and competitive tendering process was followed. Trans African Concession (TRAC) was awarded the contract as preferred bidder in December 1996 and the concession agreement was signed by TRAC in May 1997 with the Implementing Authority (IA): the Department of Transport in South Africa and the *Direccào Nacional de Estradas e Pontes* in Mozambique. The Sponsor Shareholders, who together will own 40 per cent of TRAC, are Basil Read and Stocks and Stocks (two major South African road contractors), and Bouygues, an international construction company and one of the major road builders in the world. This consortium is known as SBB.

The road is constructed on a build-operate-transfer (BOT) basis, with the concession operating for a thirty year period in agreement with the IA. The overall approach to the toll road is fully in line with the Department of Transport's White Paper, which pledged to seek out new sources for financing of transport infrastructure. According to the White Paper, 'concessions for private financing, construction, and operation, such as the Build-Operate-Transfer (BOT) agreements concluded for some major national roads, represent a method for addressing fiscal constraints within such a model' (Department of Transport, 1996). This BOT concept is part and parcel of the PPP philosophy within SDIs. The N4 toll road is a particularly good example of this as there will be no government subsidies. After the construction phase of three and a half years, funded through debt and equity raised by the concession company, as well as a certain amount of project revenue, the cost of upgrading, maintenance and operation of the road will be raised from project revenues. This will be in the form of tolling at strategically located tolling plazas.

The actual road varies from a single lane to four lanes. Whilst parts of the existing road have been simply renovated, considerable widening, for instance on the road (1.5km) as it approaches Ressano Garcia, has been conducted. In addition, as has been said, a brand new road from Moamba to Maputo is to be built, cutting out the longer 70km route from Moamba *via* Boane to Maputo. This has already been of benefit for people separated by the border, and has cut down the amount of time families need to travel to visit one another. Furthermore, the mayor of Komatipoort has taken advantage of improved transport links and negotiated an informal agreement whereby people in Ressano Garcia can now go to hospital in Komatipoort rather than Maputo.[2]

As a non-recourse funded project, financing costs needed to be borne by the revenue streams from tolls. TRAC has five toll plaza planned: (i) one near Middelburg; (ii) one at Machadodorp; (iii) one between Kaapmuiden and Malelane; (iv) one at Moamba (in Mozambique); and (v) one at Matola, just outside of Maputo. Tolling has been accepted by representatives of the road users (the Automobile Association and the Road Freight Association) as legitimate ways to maintain road services. The costing of the toll prices was taken into consideration by TRAC when bidding for the concession (DBSA, 1997: 7). The tariffs are set jointly by the National Roads Agency, TRAC as well as the lenders and shareholders of the PPP and will be increased per annum in line with inflation. This information refers to the South African side, where traffic behaviour models used in the bid were based on South African experience. Tolls on the Mozambican side replace charges previously incurred at the Mozambican-South African border and will not change the cost of a trip to Maputo. However, the toll pricing has been the subject of much controversy. On the South African side, road-users are discontented that they must now pay for using a road that was previously "free", whilst on the Mozambican side, widespread levels of poverty, as well as residual legacies from when Frelimo was socialist, mean that Mozambicans are in the main hostile to the whole PPP concept. Due to protest by local communities, TRAC has instigated a system of discounts for commuter and local users which is below (in some cases substantially below) "normal" fares.

According to the DBSA, tolls raised on the Mozambican side 'will contribute only about three to four percent of toll revenues and are not significant' (DBSA, 1997: 7). Indeed, it is apparent that South African road users are effectively subsidising Mozambican users of the toll road on the Mozambican side. Not only that, but travellers between Witbank and Middelburg are effectively subsidising other road users further east.[3] The viability of this as a method to offset costs is dependent upon traffic flows through the various toll plazas. In its planning stage, models were used to test for interest rate fluctuations, construction costs overruns, different traffic projections etc. However, there is some confusion regarding the predicated traffic flows, which may well be problematic.

Identifiable Problems

A number of problems with the toll road and its overall enabling environment have been identified. It is apparent that a great deal of high expectations were built around the road project as part of the wider MDC. 'Too high expectations were raised through premature announcements: the build-up was too much.'[4] According to one Mozambican source, the MDC concept was 'over-enthusiastic at the beginning and did not establish legal and institutional mechanisms before the project began'.[5] The conclusion was that it 'would have been much better to wait'. Whilst the promotion of the MDC was obviously necessary and a certain amount of over-selling was perhaps required, more realistic evaluations of what was possible would have been better advised. Exaggerating the potential and readiness of the MDC to receive investment has lead to disappointment on the part of prospective investors who may be reluctant to return (when the MDC is actually ready for them) if turned away at their first expression of interest. Exaggerating what the PPP contractors can or will provide to the local community is also highly problematic: there is a limitation to what TRAC can realistically do (or be expected to do).

The slow manner in which the port at Maputo has been renovated has been a major stumbling block on the success of the MDC and has impacted negatively on the flow of traffic using the N4 toll road—with hugely negative implications for the short-term financial success of the PPP. This is particularly so when the port has been characterised as 'the keyhole to the success of the Corridor'.[6] Traditionally, the port has carried a huge volume of traffic, servicing the South African hinterland and handling around 14 million tons per annum. However, the destabilisation campaign by South Africa, as well as managerial incompetence, theft and general economic and infrastructural decline, led to a situation in June 1996 where only 1.6 million tons was being handled. Renovating the port and resurrecting its capacity is thus a crucial aspect of the broader MDC. Unfortunately, there seems to be lack of momentum in reconstructing the port. This has centred on disputes between Spoornet and the Mozambican Ports and Railway Company (CFM) which has slowed down the project. Spoornet had demanded that CFM make a substantial annual payment to Spoornet to cover operating costs, investment and technical assistance in operating the Ressano Garcia line. CFM refused and talks were suspended between the two parties. This impasse has now been broken. The privatisation deal was signed in late March, 2003 with the Maputo Port Development Company (MPDC), which will assume responsibility for managing the port of Maputo from April 14, 2003. The contract is for an initial period of 15 years, but is subject to renewal options. MPDC is 51% owned by a consortium consisting of Merseyside Docks and Harbour Company (the UK's second-largest port group), Skanska AB of Sweden and *Liscont Operadores de Contentores SA* of Portugal. The remaining 49% is owned by the government and CFM.

Yet, it seems strange that the road project (including the introduction of tolling) was rushed ahead whilst the very anchor to the overall MDC lagged behind. Obviously, the N4 PPP needed to go ahead as part of the overall MDC programme, but without an operating port at Maputo the success or otherwise of the MDC is profoundly compromised. In this sense the project went about it the wrong way: the port should have first been renovated and brought on-line, *then* the road and other associated projects would have fitted into place in a coherent and integrated manner. Tolling an existing road and reconstructing another without tackling the obvious bottleneck does not make sense. Indeed, as it stands the N4 PPP appears to be just a road, and not a development corridor.

Connected to the port at Maputo, the delays could have possibly been avoided—or at least minimised—if a pro-active involvement by the two states had attempted more forcefully to broker a deal, particularly if it had actively facilitated negotiations, recognising the importance the port has for the overall success of the MDC. This relates to a degree to the next point: in fieldwork conducted within the Corridor, every single interviewee on the South African side expressed dismay and deep disquiet about the provincial leadership in Mpumalanga. This relates to the change in leadership within the province and the ouster of Matthews Phosa as Premier, being replaced by Ndaweni Mahlangu. Phosa was widely seen as being a major political power supporting the MDC and a positive and active spirit pushing forward the project, particularly at the provincial level.

However, Phosa's replacement following inter-ANC politicking had a decidedly negative effect on the MDC. This is largely due to the activities of Mahlangu: 'his infamous statement that it is sometimes acceptable for a politician to lie has poured scorn on a province which needs good governance to raise its image as one of Africa's most desirable investment destinations' (*Mpumalanga and Maputo Corridor Report*, 4th Quarter, 1999: 10). Mahlangu's capacity as a provincial premier has been, and remains, under intense scrutiny. Not only did Mahlangu project a negative image of the province, with serious implications for investment flows into Mpumalanga, he also apparently tried to undermine the MDC as a means by which Phosa's legacy could be attacked. One interviewee claimed that Mahlangu was actively trying to derail the MDC as a means to eradicate Phosa's contribution to the province. According to this source, competence and support for the MDC declined massively post-Phosa and there was now a lack of interest and vision in regional integration. This is a major problem, particularly as a strong and competent provincial involvement is needed in the MDC in order to deal with issues surrounding cross-border co-operation.[7]

The activities of local politicians and their populist grandstanding was also found to be problematic. For instance, it was reported by one (well-informed) source that local ANC politicians had addressed meetings where they announced that the government would make sure that local users no longer had to pay the toll fees. If true, this activity breaks the concessional contract which states that 'any action by the States, the effect of which is to discriminate against this project in relation to other roads and which has a material adverse effect on the rights, interests or obligations of the concessionaire and/or results in any actual or prospective change in the concessionaire's costs or revenues, shall be deemed to be a material adverse government action and therefore the concessionaire is protected against such action' (DBSA, 1997: 24). Overall, the behaviour and activities of a number of provincial politicians has not met acceptable standards of good governance. This, and low capacity at national and provincial levels in implementing policy has, and continues to threaten to, impact negatively on the MDC and by extension the viability of the N4 PPP.

In addition, a lack of information regarding the tolling process impacted negatively on local perceptions of the PPP. According to one source, there has been a 'complete misunderstanding of the PPP process and who's it for'.[8] This has been compounded by the lack of openness regarding the concession agreement, with one source claiming that the national government refused the provincial (Mpumalanga) authorities access to the agreement.[9] A Mozambican source agreed, asserting that the concession was 'secret' and not publicly available.[10] This may be a residue of the old-style government-by-decree characteristic of the apartheid administration, but even with such information, it is apparent that there are public sections who cannot/will not accept the payment of tolls to use the road. As mentioned, those on the South African side see no radical improvements on what was already an acceptable road, whilst those in Mozambique in the main do not have the available capital, nor inclination, to pay. Indeed, on the Mozambican side this issue has become particularly acute around the siting of the toll road outside of Maputo (in Matola). One Mozambican source claimed that if the toll plaza was situated between Matola and Maputo (thereby catching daily commuters travelling from Matola to Maputo), then 'serious problems' would emerge, including the possibility of sabotage. Apparently 'all people in Matola are critical of the toll road'.[11]

On the South African side, many local residents were outraged that placing tolls on the N4 would separate them from their schools, jobs and the main shopping centres in Nelspruit. According to the local Federated Long and Local Distance Taxi Association, the 'organisation [was] not invited to any decision-making meetings about the toll gates' (*Mail and Guardian*, Johannesburg, 15 June, 1998). After a protracted dispute with the operators of the toll route, concessions were granted to local residents, who now pay reduced (though the prices remain disputed) rates for using the N4 (*African Eye News Service*, Nelspruit, 7 October, 1999). This is remarkable in that the prices seem to have been imposed upon locals arbitrarily, with little regard for the social implications of such financial impositions. Though the operators have backed down, it seems peculiar that though the MDC is predicated upon "development", its supposed beneficiaries are sidelined.

Having said this, it is apparent that TRAC has been placed in a most difficult situation. TRAC is a profit-making enterprise, yet it has had to justify its tolling activities whilst the national and provincial authorities have seemingly melted away into the background, perhaps seeking to duck responsibility for their own policies and backing of the PPP, now that their constituencies have "woken up" to the various implications. According to one source 'government has effectively pulled out and the project is really in the hands of the private sector'.[12] Yet, the PPP concept does not mean a total abdication of responsibilities by the state, either to its social constituencies or, its private sector partners. In fact, TRAC has made numerous concessions to the local communities regarding toll pricing. For instance, the tariffs approved by the governments in the bidding process were actually way above what TRAC is actually charging. This has led to questions of unsustainability being asked, particularly when the traffic flows have been less than what TRAC had predicted in its tendering documents.[13]

In addition, it must be added that civil society has not always responded to invitations to negotiate the implications of raising tolls on roads. According to one Mozambican source, the government called meetings to discuss the MDC but a number of stakeholders did not bother to attend the meetings or came unprepared. These people (primarily entrepreneurs and local companies) then complained loudly at the impact of the MDC on their businesses.[14] It is apparent that dialogue with civil society is a two-way process and more complicated than simply critiquing the state for a lack of engagement.

Having said that, the emphasis on speed within the SDI methodology precludes serious or in-depth engagement with stakeholders outside of the financial sector. One Mozambican source claimed that a lack of participation by local communities in the toll road process led to a loss of land with very little compensation and with no job creation. This then led to indignation and opposition against the PPP.[15] This may spring from the overall fast-track approach to the SDI concept (see De Beer and Arkwright, chapter 2; Söderbaum, chapter 5). According to one source, 'the Department of Trade and Industry (DTI), the government's custodian of GEAR and its SDI-offshoots, has taken a hard line and non-negotiable stand on the planning of SDI projects, particularly when it comes to issues of grassroots participation, given the fast-track nature of the SDI processes' (Moloi, 1998: 16). Certainly, the implementation of a fast-track approach in Mozambique caused problems in an environment where capacity to evaluate the implications of projects was limited at the best of times.[16]

Lessons for other SDIs

Fundamental to any successful implementation of a PPP is the commercial viability of the project. The MDC makes economic sense and is potentially workable and profitable (though traffic flows and a lack of other development along the MDC may threaten the N4 PPP). In fact, the very workability of the N4 PPP may be dependent upon the fact that it is being built around an already existing infrastructure and not the actual viability of the PPP approach *per se*. Having said this, the list of other proposed SDIs is problematic and needs a careful re-thought if PPPs are to be invited. The SDI philosophy and its attendant notion of PPPs is not and should not be, buzzwords or the latest fad. The viability of a number of proposed SDIs is doubtful and should be re-examined. It is axiomatic that good infrastructure bases are needed for any good development project if it is based on the SDI concept. A number of SDIs in the pipeline do not have this and are unlikely to attract substantial or realistic PPP contractors.

Introducing PPPs requires a favourable macroeconomic climate and a regulatory framework that supports and encourages private sector involvement. South Africa and Mozambique currently have this, despite rising criticism of the neo-liberal framework used to construct such a "favourable climate". However, wayward comments by politicians have at times undermined this confidence. In particular, the manner in which provincial politicians have at times conducted themselves in Mpumalanga is not conducive to a successful SDI and has on occasion directly challenged the whole PPP idea. Future PPPs within SDIs must be totally backed by national and provincial government and maverick behaviour by politicians and/or public officials dealt with speedily and openly. If this is not done, investor confidence and willingness to engage in PPPs is (understandably) compromised.

In addition, future PPPs need a firm commitment on the part of the state to provide support for private actors and agree on a set list of responsibilities. The state must not abandon private investors to the vagaries of political opinion: it is not the job of PPP contractors to sort out political problems. Rather, this should be left to the politicians. This of course is not a one-way street and the private sector needs to understand its social responsibilities. On this point it is important to stress that the private sector does have social responsibilities and that recent thinking has acknowledged this important fact. On this point, it is imperative that both the South African and Mozambican governments *compel, monitor and enforce* empowerment and developmental obligations undertaken by contracting capital ventures. A "big-bang" and then hands-off approach mitigates against such surveillance and needs to be re-thought (see Söderbaum and Taylor, chapter 4). By doing so both the public and private sector will be held accountable to their constituencies and held to the social commitments they have already articulated. This can actually benefit the private contractor in the PPP as if it is demonstrated to local communities that the PPP has practical advantages, support is likely to be sustained.

Specific contractual obligations to involve local partners on the ground, particularly those managed by and with a strong labour component comprised of disadvantaged persons, such as blacks and women, would be vital to any positive spin-offs from private sector involvement. Admittedly, if this is realised the capacity to monitor the social implications of the MDC may well be lacking at certain junctures, but serious attempts to do so are vital. The very low level of Mozambican NGO activity regarding the MDC however is problematic on this score and needs addressing.[17] The role of international donors may well play a part here.

Whilst the N4 toll road is an example of PPPs "in action", the problems raised above indicate that they are not a panacea to Africa's developmental impasse. Whilst the ECA has hinged a great deal on promoting PPPs as a new model for Africa, actually-existing PPPs such as the N4 road suggests that a myriad of factors preclude this model from being adopted willy-nilly throughout the continent. It would be a mistake if the PPP "philosophy" was taken on board by the ECA as the new "one-size-fits-all" programme as we have observed with many Structural Adjustment Programmes. The ECA has clearly bought into the neo-liberal discourse, as have the proponents of the SDI and PPP. That this reflects the hegemony of a particular developmental approach reflects the power that liberalising globalisation has in the minds and actions of elites throughout the world—Africa included. Whilst the PPP approach may offer partial solutions to promoting growth and *some* development in the continent, a more careful appraisal of the pitfalls that such projects engenders should be thought through by both the proponents of the MDC and the ECA.

Notes

1. Interview with Dr. Alfredo Namitete, Chairman, Committee of Senior Officials, Southern African Transport and Communications Commission (SATCC), Maputo, 6 April 2000.
2. Interview with Jonathan Mitchell, Special Projects and Policy Unit, Mpumalanga Province, Nelspruit, 5 April 2000.
3. Interview with Jonathan Mitchell, Special Projects and Policy Unit, Mpumalanga Province, Nelspruit, 5 April 2000.
4. Interview with Gordon Griffiths, Chief Executive Officer, Mpumalanga Investment Initiative (MII), Nelspruit, 4 April 2000.
5. Interview with Dr. Alfredo Namitete, Chairman, Committee of Senior Officials, Southern African Transport and Communications Commission (SATCC), Maputo, 6 April 2000.
6. Interview with Gordon Griffiths, Chief Executive Officer, Mpumalanga Investment Initiative (MII), Nelspruit, 4 April 2000.
7. Interview with Dave Arkwright, South African Project Manager of MDC, Nelspruit, 12 April 2000.
8. Interview with Jonathan Mitchell, Special Projects and Policy Unit, Mpumalanga Province, Nelspruit, 5 April 2000.
9. Interview with Jonathan Mitchell, Special Projects and Policy Unit, Mpumalanga Province, Nelspruit, 5 April 2000.
10. Interview with Dr. Alfredo Namitete, Chairman, Committee of Senior Officials, Southern African Transport and Communications Commission (SATCC), Maputo, 6 April 2000.
11. Interview with D. Liuzzi, co-ordinator of KULIMA non-governmental organisation, Maputo, 6 April 2000.
12. Interview with Jonathan Mitchell, Special Projects and Policy Unit, Mpumalanga Province, Nelspruit, 5 April 2000.
13. Interview with Greg White, Development Bank of Southern Africa (DBSA), Halfway House, South Africa, 14 April 2000.
14. Interview with Franscisca Soares, MDC Project Manager, Mozambican Ministry of Transport and Communications, Maputo, 10 April 2000.
15. Interview with Dr. Alfredo Namitete, Chairman, Committee of Senior Officials, Southern African Transport and Communications Commission (SATCC), Maputo, 6 April 2000.
16. Interview with Franscisca Soares, Mozambican Ministry of Transport and Communications, Maputo, 10 April 2000.
17. Interview with Milissao Nuvunga, lecturer at the *Instituto Superior de Relações Internacionais* (ISRI), Maputo, 7 April 2000.

Chapter 7

The Mozambique Aluminium Smelter: Partnership for Exploitation or Development?

James Hentz

The Mozambique aluminium smelter (Mozal) just outside Maputo anchors one end of the Maputo Development Corridor (MDC), running from Witbank in Mpumalanga to Maputo, the capital of Mozambique. The refurbished N4 toll road connects the two. The US$1.365 billion Mozal project is a classic example of what Söderbaum and Taylor (chapter 1 and 4) refer to as the "big-bang" approach to development, which is built on large-scale capital-intensive investment. The impact upon the Mozambican economy is immense—for 1998 the value added to the Mozambique economy of Mozal was estimated at 4.5 per cent of GDP (IDC, 2002). Mozal is essentially a partnership of the state and private sectors, represented respectively by Mozambique, with a four per cent interest; South Africa, through the Industrial Development Corporation (IDC), with a 24 per cent interest; and the two giant conglomerates of BHP Billiton, with 47 per cent and Mitsubishi with 25 per cent. Finally, the International Financial Corporation (IFC), contributed US$55 million and quasi-equity of US$65 million, making it at the time its largest single investment anywhere in the world.

The concept "partnership" has multiple dimensions (also see Ngwenya and Taylor, chapter 6). First, and ostensibly neutral, is the business partnership between the state and private business that is expected to promote development. Second, underlying the business partnership is a political deal, operating on multiple levels. At the domestic level in South Africa, the Mozal (and the MDC in general) is a partnership between capital and the state. In Mozambique, the absence of a well-developed capitalist class means Mozal is more a political fiat of the administrative/governing class. At the international level it is a partnership between both South Africa and Mozambique on the one hand and international capital on the other hand. The first notion, business partnership, calls to mind Rostow's (1971) classic argument that an economy would "take-off" after it reached a certain level of GDP. This economic logic however ignores the political dimension, the second dimension of the partnership, which determines who benefits.

The impact of SDIs—and more specifically the Mozal project—on regional development can be addressed from two interlocking perspectives. First, does it promote economic development? Without such development, South Africa will develop apace of its neighbours and, indeed, SDIs will look like a Constellation of Southern African States (CONSAS) redux. Second, within the political context of the ongoing global hegemony of neo-liberalism, who is empowered? We can assume that the Mozal deal benefits South Africa, or at least a fraction of it, but what does it do for Mozambique?

This chapter adopts the new regionalism approach (NRA) to explain what drives the project and for whose benefit it was built (see Söderbaum and Taylor, chapter 1). Mozal is a nodule in the complex interplay of regionalisation/ regionalism and globalisation/globalism. As part of a micro-region, Mozal connects Mozambique to the globalisation process, while weaving another strand in the southern African lattice of economic interdependence. "New regionalism", to paraphrase the editors of this volume, rejects the simple state-based ontology of mainstream approaches in the field, instead taking into account processes within and across communities, and situating such processes within the ongoing global hegemony of neo-liberalism, as both an economic and political project (Söderbaum and Taylor, chapter 4).

The focus here is on the formal side of the equation, because Mozal and the MDC are a political reality where the power of developmental discourses meet the material interests of domestic and international players. The MDC and Mozal are primarily driven by South African interests that are shaped by the logic of its own political economy, which is produced and reproduced in relation to or as part of the hegemonic project of neo-liberalism. But Mozambique, as well, has embraced the South African approach to regionalism, its underlying developmental logic, and has become a willing partner to South Africa, or at least its current political elites have.

The chapter is divided into four parts. First, it traces the support for capital-intensive projects, such as Mozal, and subsequently Mozal II, the Sasol project, and the Sands River project, to the debate in transitional South Africa over an economic growth and development strategy for post-apartheid South Africa. This debate reveals a fault-line, separating the interests of South Africa's traditional capital-intensive sectors from the interests of its labour-intensive industries, and separating their respective constituencies. SDIs and Mozal do nothing to narrow this divide. The second part of the chapter looks at SDIs within the context of South Africa's neo-liberal turn, marked by its adoption of the Growth, Employment and Redistribution (GEAR) programme and its regionalisation project. Mozal, it can be argued, is a product of South Africa's neo-liberal turn (Hentz, 1999; Taylor, 2001) and implies a reconstitution of South Africa's regional relations in a way that favours its traditional capital-intensive sector. But this does not necessarily mean a return to the apartheid era's notion of a CONSAS and in fact, we should not assume that Mozal has *no* developmental dimension. This is as much a matter of empirics as it is of theory. The third section will briefly describe Mozambique's neo-liberal turn and how Mozal will impact on its economic development. Here the focus will be on Mozambique's adoption of the "big-bang" approach, and what this kind of regionalism means for economic development in Mozambique. Finally, a conclusion rounds up the chapter.

The Way Forward: The Economic Debate in Transitional South Africa

The way forward is obviously influenced by where you start. Apartheid's legacy to the "new" South Africa is critical, because it granted pole position to South Africa's capital-intensive industries, thereby promoting the entrenched economic and political interests of the big business conglomerate sector while handicapping the labour-intensive sector. The traditional lodestar of the South African economy is its mining industry, particularly gold: it spurred both a manufacturing sector and a demand for skilled labour. But these two demands were in awkward juxtaposition throughout the apartheid era. In Lewis' (1990: 58) words, 'the most striking finding regarding the commodity composition of South Africa's exports is the early and continued dominance of gold, both as a share of total exports and as a share of GDP'. Stadler (1987: 33) argues that manufacturing had always been a weak sector, surviving by state support sieved from the mining industry. Nonetheless, South Africa's adoption of an import substitution industrialisation (ISI) strategy did lead to a shift from mining to manufacturing (Lewis, 1990: 24), and South Africa's large parastatals drove the development of its manufacturing sector. South Africa created the IDC in 1939 to attract foreign investment to fund the creation of public corporations in partnership with private businesses. However, it did so, so as not to stimulate the demand for skilled Black labour.

South Africa's giant parastatals tied manufacturing to mining. Beginning in the 1920s, the South African state encouraged the development of the manufacturing sector by establishing and providing finance through the IDC for large parastatals, such as, Iscor (iron and steel), Eskom (electricity), Sasol (fuel), Foskor (phosphate) and Mossgas (gas). In the 1970s South Africa's capital-intensive industries led the shift from an import substitution industrialisation (ISI) to export oriented industrialisation (EOI). During the 1980s, manufacturing exports grew from 27 per cent to 35 per cent of South Africa's total exports and four highly capital-intensive sectors accounted for almost half of those exports, namely, iron and steel, chemicals, non-ferrous metals, and pulp and paper (GATT, 1991: 26). While the share of total investment in chemical and basic metals grew from 40.4 per cent in 1972 to 59.8 per cent in 1990, the share in the three most labour-intensive sectors—clothing, leather and footwear, and wood and furniture—declined during the same period from 4 per cent to 1.9 per cent (Joffe et al., 1993: 95). These parastatals were imbued with the political logic of apartheid and concomitantly shaped the character of South Africa's capital-labour relations. In Nattrass' (1990: 123) words, 'South Africa's macro-economic and labour policies tended to be highly contradictory attempts to marry the requirements of capitalist growth with the demands of capitalists, White workers, and an ideology of racial segregation'. And Clark (1994: 10) states, 'advanced technology has allowed South African state enterprises to avoid the use of labour that was reputed to be cheap but would in fact have entailed substantial [political] costs'. Therefore, government policies such as the Physical Planning Act and state-supported investments in capital-intensive industry were central to both the ISI strategy and to the move towards EOI (Black, 1993: 230); which essentially amounted to a survival strategy for South Africa's conglomerate and parastatal sector. The late 1970s to 1980s export drive was, in fact, meant to support capital-intensive industry. The post-apartheid economic plan was imbedded in the same logic.

This apartheid legacy shaped transitional South Africa's industrialisation and trade debate. That debate was framed by the issue of what industries should be the future engines of growth. The underlying purpose of South Africa's early rounds of economic liberalisation was to increase the competitiveness of its industries, but how competitiveness was defined in transitional South Africa also determined what industries were considered competitive. This would provide the rational for projects such as Mozal. During the transition, revealed comparative advantage was the dominant approach for determining competitiveness. However, as Hirsch claimed, 'perhaps the most serious problem is that comparative advantage analysis can only measure the results of trade. Therefore they cannot compensate for policy biases built into the trade regime and yield some "true" comparative advantage indicator' (Hirsch, 1993: 85).

This problem had important political implications. Policy biases are grounded in political logic, and in transitional South Africa this led to emphasising its traditional export strength in resource-based and large-scale projects. The supporting argument was that these sorts of projects, namely the Columbus Stainless Steel Development and the Alusaf Aluminium Project, would provide a trickle-down effect for the rest of the economy. This is the exact same argument used to defend the proposition that Mozal will foster development. These large projects, traditionally the product of IDC funding, as is Mozal, were expected to earn foreign exchange, increase savings, and avoid the problem of high labour costs. Pagel (1992: 49), for instance, argued that an analysis of South Africa's comparative advantage by sector shows that 'although various criteria, statistical methods and different sources were used over the years, the following manufacturing sectors invariably show promising signs in terms of potential for increased exports based on international competitiveness. These sectors are iron and steel, metal, chemical, and wood and pulp paper'.

Large corporations and parastatals dominated these sectors. The IDC (1993: 2), a major stakeholder in Mozal, concluded, 'substantial investment in large projects such as aluminium, stainless steel and heavy minerals production were announced recently, capitalising on South Africa's international competitiveness in minerals and energy'. Therefore, the revealed comparative advantage approach, regardless of its academic merit, had powerful underlying political inferences in transitional South Africa. It framed the debate so that capital-intensive industry would naturally not only take centre stage in South Africa, but also shove labour-intensive industry off that stage. Osborn (1992) stated, 'these enterprises [large capital-intensive] have appropriate marketing organisation with the necessary expertise in exporting, and there is little reliance on official marketing support.

Furthermore, their export performance is related to the conditions of the foreign market and not to the presence of any export incentive scheme'. This is coded language for taking the state out of the development equation, but beneath the neutral language of economic development is the political question of development for whom? Labour, of course, saw a different picture.

As representative of labour's views, the COSATU (Congress of South African Trade Unions)-sponsored Industrial Strategy Project (ISP), on the other hand, argued that where most of South Africa's investment had gone during the apartheid era, namely chemicals and steel, job creation had been minimal. It argued that job creation would be better in footwear and clothing (ISP, 1993: 5). These products would be included in what Hirsch (1993) labelled 'narrow manufactures', which excluded semi-manufactured exports such as chemicals, iron and steel, and wood pulp. Hirsch pointed out that between 1988 and 1991, exports of 'narrow manufactures' doubled, although admittedly they were still at a very low level. The greatest improvement came in 'other transport equipment', 'autos and parts' and 'clothing' (Hirsch, 1993: 73).

Because transitional South Africa witnessed a bifurcation in trade policy preferences, between support for more labour-intensive industry and the traditional capital-intensive sectors, it engendered a re-examination of trade promotion policies. The beneficiaries of the *status quo*, big business, favoured the old policies, or possibly a "level playing field", because they could capitalise on their pole-position. Labour and small business would logically favour changes in South Africa's trade policy. The divide between big business and labour (and small enterprises) was superimposed on the regional grid. In fact, given the importance of the regional market during the decades of formal isolation, regional trade relations were politically charged.

GEAR, SDIs and Mozal in Context

The ANC came to power in 1994 with an ostensibly Keynesian economic platform and the state was expected to play a major role. In fact, the ANC threatened to reverse the privatisation programme begun with the 1987 White Paper on Privatisation and Deregulation in the Republic of South Africa. Iscor had been privatised in 1989, National Sorghum in 1991, others were to follow. As I have argued elsewhere, the privatisation drive was, however, grounded in the National Party's exit strategy, and in the sectoral competition within transitional South Africa's political economy (Hentz, 2000a).

However, while the Reconstruction and Development Programme (RDP) reflected the issues (housing, training, services, and jobs) important to the ANC's base constituency, the ANC's macroeconomic policies after the April 1994 elections were characterised as both moderate and business friendly. Characterisations of the ANC leadership are illustrative. Jay Naidoo, the ex-head of COSATU, and the new government's Minister in charge of implementing the RDP was once described as, 'looking like Satan, sounding like Marx, and acting like

Mephistopheles'. As Minister he was described as 'a figure of flawless economic orthodoxy'. Alec Erwin, the new government's Deputy Minister of Finance and an ex-unionist, was labelled 'a convert to economic orthodoxy' (*Financial Times*, Johannesburg, 18 July 1994). In Mandela's first *State of the Union* address in front of Parliament, he was as intent on soothing the fears of foreign investors and domestic business, as in pleasing his traditional supporters (*Associated Press*, Cape Town, 24 May 1994). In the opening session of the World Economic Forum in Cape Town in June 1994, Mandela stressed that his government would adhere to Western economic policies rather than the socialist policies the ANC advocated as a banned liberation movement (*Associated Press*, Cape Town, 9 June 1994).

The culmination of South Africa's shift to neo-liberal economic policies was the 1996 GEAR programme. GEAR, Hein Marais explained, included justification for the privatisation drive begun in the 1980s (Marais, 1998: 163). It was meant to send a signal to international financial markets that South Africa was investment friendly. It is GEAR's commitment to attracting foreign investment and its export orientation that earned it the neo-liberal label, and the SDIs and therefore Mozal, should be seen as tied to GEAR. Legum (2000: 17-8), for instance, states that through GEAR the South African government has encouraged SDIs, such as the MDC and the Mozal. Jourdan (1998: 718) has made it clear that the SDIs are about investment, arguing that the two main strategies are to 'remove bottlenecks to investment' and to 'identify strategic investment opportunities' (see Söderbaum and Taylor, chapter 4). Thus, Tessely (2001: 4) can argue that SDIs suit the neo-liberal paradigm of development. However, South Africa's economic policy is not completely congruent with neo-liberal orthodoxy, at least not from the perspective of economic policy.

The dependence on various types of public-private partnerships (PPPs) is consistent with long established practices in South Africa. The IDC's role in Mozal is the application at the regional level of what it has done at the domestic level since its creation in 1939. In fact, during the transition Hirsch (1993: 19) called South Africa's new tilt towards industrial policy with protection the 'neo-structuralist' position, and he argued that the Normative Economic Programme (NEM) of 1993 demonstrated its growing influence in government. Even the South African Chamber of Business (SACOB), favoured an 'industrial policy', albeit it argued that industrial policy should not cater to 'unsustainable employment' (SACOB, 1993: 19). As one analyst stated at the time, the very success of the IDC demonstrated the success of this approach (Black, 1993: 231).

The SDIs, therefore, represent the marriage of an aggressive industrial policy and a particular form of regional economic integration. In Lewis and Bloch's words, the methodology 'is explicitly designed to support the focus of the government's industrial policy on export growth, to underpin the industrialisation of the southern Africa region's nation states and to promote southern African regional integration' (Lewis and Bloch, 1998: 730). But, as well, from South Africa's perspective Lewis and Bloch add, SDIs 'simultaneously further reinforce the highly capital intensive, natural resource-based character of our [South African] manufacturing sector' (Lewis and Bloch, 1998: 732; see also Tessely, 2001; Bond,

2000; and Jourdan, 1998). The point is, while large capital-intensive projects like Mozal are firmly embedded in the globalisation of the region, they are also a hybrid of neo-liberal orthodoxy and industrial policy adopted by the governments in the region. Whether the partnership(s) leads to development or rather exploitation cannot be answered by labelling them but instead, I would suggest, by understanding the politics of the partnership(s). There are domestic, regional and international partnerships involved.

Legum (2000: 17) describes post-apartheid regionalisation as: 'a constellation of Southern African economies led by private capital', a slightly veiled reference to CONSAS. However, this sticks not only because of the strength of the capital-intensive sector within South Africa but also because with the help of the IFIs South Africa could tap into the lucrative big project business. South Africa was certainly well positioned to dominate infrastructure development in post-apartheid southern Africa. The Southern African Development Community (SADC) had, in fact, expressed concern over South Africa's ability to dominate externally funded projects in their member states. An African Development Bank (ADB) study, as well, cautioned that South African business perceives re-entry to regional markets as an advantage only so much as it enables them to compete for aid-funded contracts and expand aid-funded exports (ADB, 1992: 1-2). The importance of World Bank contracts to South Africa and South Africa's regional dominance in procuring contracts took off during the transition. From 1 July 1992 to 30 June 1993, South Africa was awarded thirty-three contracts in southern Africa (Lesotho 9, Malawi 5, Mozambique 8, Zambia 5, Zimbabwe 6); no other country in the region was awarded a contract for a country outside its own borders. In fact, the South African total in dollars for the region was close to the total sum for all the other countries (except South Africa) in the region. As South Africa prepared to formalise regional relations, capital-intensive industries had already gained a firm foothold in the subcontinent. Indeed, SADC has largely been left out of the SDI loop and the 'powerful bilateral processes' driving the SDIs foster suspicion by multilateral organisations (Mitchell, 1998: 758; Söderbaum, and Taylor, 2002: 682).

Mozal and Mozambique: Why, and for Whom?

If SDIs and Mozal are part of South Africa's neo-liberal turn they are also part of Mozambique's neo-liberal conversion too and tie in with Mozambique's own structural adjustment programme, the *Programa de Reabilitação Nacional* (PRE). Mozambique's Fifth National Congress in 1989 signalled the end of its socialist experiment (Simpson, 1993: 331). Part of this abandonment includes rapid privatisation, and since 1985 Mozambique has sold 340 small, medium and large-sized state companies from all sectors of the economy (Pitcher, 1996: 49). The major opposing parties of Mozambique's National Assembly, Frelimo and Renamo, support privatisation (Pitcher, 1996: 50).

Therefore, as with South Africa, the neo-liberal turn in Mozambique has a domestic political dimension. Frelimo, the party that has ruled Mozambique since independence, originally had the classic post-independent African urban bias—the countryside was downgraded and peasant farmers exploited for the benefit of its urban constituency (Simpson, 1993: 326). Privatisation, the central element of Mozambique's current development policies had domestic and international elements. Domestically, it was a way for Frelimo to cut into Renamo's support base in the centre and north of the country (Pitcher, 1996: 55). It is also meant to nurture a national bourgeoisie (Simpson, 1993: 334). But, in conjunction with structural adjustment, the PRE. has alienated urban classes. In particular, the Organization of Mozambican Workers (OTM) has rebelled (Simpson, 1993: 224).

The international dimension to Mozambique's neo-liberal turn locks it into globalisation. First, it has been highly dependent on external aid: 79 per cent of its foreign exchange earnings in 1988 were from foreign aid (Pitcher, 1996: 54). Second, as it made the transition to a privatised economy, indigenous businesses lacked the necessary accumulated capital and access to credits (Torp and Rekve, 1998: 83). International backing, for instance in the privatisation of the cotton industry (Pitcher, 1996: 63), was therefore essential. Similarly, Mozal is meant to fix the economy, or at least start it on its way.

From the perspective of a foreign direct investment (FDI) starved country, Mozal is a success. The project is also seen as a model of business/finance success. The Harvard Business School and the Darden Business School at the University of Virginia use it as a case study. In fact, the project came in approximately US$130 million under-cost and six months ahead of schedule. But, is it a *development* project? It should be remarked that Kimura and Husain of the International Finance Corporation (IFC) recommended approval of the project based on its 'significant economic and developmental benefits' (Harvard Business School, 2000: 1). Five criteria can be used to judge Mozal's developmental impact: job creation; down-stream and up-stream benefits; Hirschman's 'centrality of side effects', i.e. development of the bureaucracy (state capacity); what Söderbaum and Taylor call 'ownership' of the process (2001: 69); and empowerment. The SDIs, and therefore Mozal, have four stated objectives: to rehabilitate the core infrastructure; to maximise investment; to ensure that the development impact is maximised, particularly to disadvantaged communities; and to ensure sustainability. The first two have been largely successful, so the developmental impact rests with the latter two, which closely track the criteria 1-4 suggested above (see De Beer and Arkwright, chapter 2; Söderbaum and Taylor, chapter 4).

Development and Employment Creation

Given its capital-intensive character, the MDC and Mozal is most often challenged for its potential for providing jobs (Mitchell, 1998: 764), particularly given a 45 per cent unemployment rate in Mozambique at its initiation (IFC, 1997). Importantly, SDIs are claimed to boost employment and to encourage Black empowerment. The construction stage employed up to 9,000 workers (65 per cent Mozambicans); the permanent workforce, thereafter, was approximately 900; and 5,000 workers were trained by Mozal (IDC, 2002). Paul Jourdan, the lead South African official in charge of the SDI initiative, claimed there would be a three to five times multiplier effect (*Weekly Mail and Guardian*, Johannesburg, 18 September 1998), although multipliers were not as great as expected. The IDC estimated indirect job opportunities at 2,500 (IDC, 2002), and Mozal has been credited with creating 3,500 secondary jobs.

The possible down-stream spin-offs for Mozal were not expected to be significant, but as it imports practically all its materials, and exports the final product, it did lead to infrastructural developments, such as two power transmission lines; a) road network and bridges; telecommunications systems; water supply/pipelines, sewerage and draining systems; new Matola harbour facilities; and an enhanced Maputo port. Of these, the Maputo port may be the most significant. Mozal has already significantly increased the tonnage going out of Maputo port, but more important for job creation, for every new job at the port there are four new direct spin-off jobs and ten indirect jobs created, and these jobs are more concentrated in SMMEs than are Mozal's spin-off jobs. Privatisation, however, also means retrenchment. The Mozambique Ports and Railways is the major employer in the country, and job loss will impact villages all along the railway.[1] The World Bank has given US$8 million for "rationalisation".

The construction stage of Mozal obviously accounted for much more direct employment than the operations stage, albeit they are temporary jobs. This can be ameliorated if Mozal attracts new investment into Mozambique. And, in fact, two or three large (capital-intensive projects) are in the pipeline. The US$1 billion Mozal II project is the first, projected to double the aluminium smelting capacity. Two other mega-projects are expected to follow, the Sasol pipeline that will transport natural gas from Mozambique to South Africa, and the Corridor Sands (titanium) project. There are also plans for a Beluluane Industrial Park (BIP)—where Mozal is located—which will create an estimated 20,000 jobs (IDC, 2002; De Beer and Arkwright, chapter 2). Thus, although construction jobs are by definition temporary, there may be a growing demand for construction workers, particularly for ones who gained skills on-the-job in prior projects. Interestingly, the Director General of Mozal, Peter Wilshaw, noted that they had anticipated a 60 per cent return of the original workforce from Mozal I for Mozal II, but have only actually generated a 40 per cent return.[2]

Mitchell (1998: 768), in what is otherwise a fairly critical assessment of the MDC, states that the 'role in maximising secondary investment in the corridor area appears to be very successful in Mozambique'. There appears to be a learning curve here. Lewis and Bloch (1998: 747) state that the Saldanha Steel project has done much better in growth and development objectives (subcontracting, materials procurement), than has Richards Bay. The latter, also a large aluminium smelter, is often the benchmark for large capital-intensive investments. The emphasis on partnerships between local businesses and Mozal is international, for instance, through the Africa Project Development Faculty, the IFC is providing capacity-building support for local businesses to expand their role as contractors to Mozal (IFC, 2001). Mozambique's Investment Promotion Centre (CPI) has set up a one-stop-shop to facilitate the participation of local SMMEs. Approximately 100 local companies supply Mozal, with a total of approximately US$22 million a year in business.[3]

Development and the Creation of State Capacity

What are the intangibles? These are defined as not directly tied to the profit motive. Two groupings can be considered: spin-off developmental projects and state capacity. However, they are, within the Mozal scheme, incidental. This is difficult terrain to traverse so a short introduction is necessary. Both the management of Mozal and people involved with the project at the IDC in South Africa make no excuses for the profit motive underlying Mozal. They make it clear that their constituency is the shareholders. However, conversations with these officials are replete with the language of development, that is, "sustainable development". It would be unfair to assume that Mozal's efforts in support of "sustainable development" are disingenuous, but their structures can be examined purely analytically and they seem to mimic the "take-off" logic of Mozal.

As part of the financing package, the Mozal Community Development Trust (MCDT), was created. It is financed, largely, from a one per cent of pre-profit tax donated by Mozal.[4] Included in its portfolio are an HIV/Aids awareness programme; the Lubombo Malaria Protocol; the building of local schools; a new local health clinic; a business skills training programme; training of 1,200 local farmers; housing; a food processing centre; a police station; and assistance to a local brick-builder. In some cases these projects have additional external financing, i.e. from the Development Bank of Southern Africa (DBSA). But, there is an important caveat. Mozal's commitment is not open-ended. After a time, these projects, and by inference future funding, are expected to be self-sustaining. This is what is meant by the devolution of responsibility to the local level. After a period of time, to be determined by Mozal, development will devolve back to the state and the local authorities. For sure, there is little or no effort on the part of the Mozambican state to codify Mozal's responsibility to the community. To be fair, thus far Mozal has been a good member of the community, but moving to the local level will be difficult. First, SDIs and Mozal specifically, are dominated at the national level, and in particular by South Africa (De Beer and Arkwright, chapter 2). Even Mpumalanga province in South Africa, the local authority responsible for the MDC (in theory), has no plan or strategy to take over (see Söderbaum, chapter 5).

Mozal has been credited with increasing state capacity. A top level official at the CPI, a government organisation under the Ministry of Finance, emphasised that they have had to become more professional and efficient because of their interaction with Mozal and foreign investors.[5] In fact, almost every government official the author interviewed in May 2002 volunteered that dealing at such a high level had forced Mozambican bureaucrats to be more professional. This may have even impacted on corruption. This is interesting as Harrison (1999: 545) argues that Mozambique's liberalisation has led to increased corruption and he specifically mentions customs corruption. But, because Mozal imports all the raw materials for the smelter, its customs department has had to become more professional. This began at the legislative level.[6] There is also anecdotal evidence that the customs offices are becoming more professional and less corrupt.[7] Finally, Mozambique's commercial law has been credited with increasing state capacity.[8]

Globalisation and Empowerment: Labour's Response

Mozal's developmental impact, tangible and intangible, cannot be ignored, but neither can it be understood outside the context of globalisation. Mozal represents a deal between local political elite and transnational capital. This is not the place to review the vast literature on globalisation, but Mozal is a classic example of how the process works: Mozal is an industrial free zone; pays tax at one per cent of turnover; is exempt from customs duties, sales and circulation tax; and its staff get a 40 per cent reduction on their income tax bill. The IDC estimates the revenues to be: US$4.1 million per annum from the one per cent levy on turnover; and US$5 million per annum due to Mozambique's four per cent ownership (IDC, 2002). When put into the context of ownership, it is easy to guess where most of the profit goes, and not only do the major shareholders reap much of the profit, but giant South Africa firms like Murray and Roberts and LTA, and the energy company, Eskom, are also positioned to benefit. In fact, the giant South African energy parastatal, Eskom, was the catalyst for Mozal as it wanted to utilise some of its surplus capacity (Harvard Business School, 2000: 2). Because electricity was 25 per cent of the total production costs, electricity was the most important determinant of Mozal's competitive position.

As Woods (1999: 25) states, globalisation is about 'meta-power or who gets to make the rules within which international relations proceed and who decides how and where to enforce them'. SDIs, the MDC and Mozal as exemplars send a political message that may be deeper and more powerful than their developmental potential. In South Africa's case, they reinforce the dominance of its large conglomerate and parastatal sectors, which includes the financial sector. Thus, while South Africa provided export financing in the form of export credit, US$700 million of which US$380 million was by the Government,[9] it served the already dominant capital-intensive conglomerates. In Mozambique's case, a nascent elite is forming around the meta-projects and their government backers (Söderbaum and Taylor, chapter 4). In fact, the Frelimo government's neo-liberal turn has important political implications. As in South Africa, Mozambique's structural adjustment has alienated labour. This should come as no surprise because as Rodrik (1997: 545) points out, globalisation shifts the distribution of the tax burden from capital to labour.

It needs to be recognised that Mozambique's distressed working class has challenged the political power of the management class. On 3 October 2001, Mozal workers, members of the National Union of Metal and Energy Workers (SINTIME), went on strike. The "legality" of this strike has been questioned, but its underlying causes and subsequent settlement underscore the politics of globalisation. Mozal immediately fired 700 metalworkers, calling in police and dogs to clear them out (*News and Letters*, Maputo, November 2001). The General Director of Mozal gave three reasons for the strike: workers were over-extended in dollar denominated loans (i.e. for new cars); there was a significant difference between local wages and expatriate wages (i.e. South African workers); and the industrial free zone legislature had diluted their rights.[10] Each of these causes is specific to Mozal and representative of a larger struggle. The "dollarisation" of Mozambique's economy is a problem—while loans taken out for cars were denominated in hard currency, the workers are paid in local currency and medical benefits are tied to the dollar.[11] As in much of the developing word, the depreciation of local currencies creates a debt-trap, in this case a personal one. The fact that expatriate workers were paid more for the same work made things worse; on average the expatriates were paid three times the local wage with a monthly "malaria allowance". Finally, Mozambique had revamped its labour law to be more "free market friendly", and Mozal had negotiated an agreement limiting workers' right to strike.

The Mozambican union SINTIME went to Mozal with "discussion points" before the strike. There were two main components: a salary increase and medical insurance (SINTIME, *Communications Brief: Human Resources*, 17/12/2001). The salary increase was indexed to inflation, calibrated in local inflation rates on the American consumer price index. The medical insurance was 'to ensure that all out employees and their immediate families are protected regarding their health for a better quality of life' (SINTIME, *Communications Brief: Human Resources*, 17/12/2001). Mozal refused to negotiate. As explained by Alfredo Guiamba, Secretary-General of SINTIME, the labour agreement stipulated that you could not strike when negotiating, so by refusing to negotiate Mozal precipitated the strike.[12] Of a total of approximately 700 workers, 468 went on strike. All but forty were taken back. These last have to go through legal hearings to get reinstated, at an official pace of about two a week. In practice, however, only one hearing a week has been scheduled. From the perspective of SINTIME, this is a way to isolate and intimidate the workers (SINTIME, *Communications Brief: Human Resources*, 17/12/2001).

SINTIME did not have to stand alone. It got strong support form the International Metalworkers Federation (IMF) and from the National Union of Metal South Africa (NUMSA). Metalworkers in South Africa called for a solidarity strike, although, it never materialised. Nonetheless, the sentiment reflected in the words of one South African metalworker at a Billiton plant is revealing: 'Capital has never respected borders. We are starting to do the same' (*News and Letters*, Maputo, November 2001).

The agreement after the strike was at least a partial victory for SINTIME. The purchasing power component (PPC) was increased, there was a salary increase, and housing and medical benefits were improved. However, the larger meta-issues—that is, the right to strike—are unresolved.

The economics of Mozal may lead to indeterminate conclusions as to its developmental credentials. The IFC claims that the benefit to Mozambique was good (Harvard Business School, 2000: 7). The politics of Mozal are clear—imbedded in the push and pull of globalisation, Mozal is part of the 'increasing legitimacy and spread of market-based systems for allocation and exchange within and between countries' (Prakash and Hart, 1999: 7). This is a political project led by factions within both South Africa and Mozambique that stand to benefit most from untethered markets (see Söderbaum and Taylor, chapter 4).

Conclusion

Mozal must be considered as a two-dimensional process, *economic development* and *regionalisation*, each driven by political logic. From an *economic development* perspective Mozal is formally a developmental project. It does not, necessarily, represent neo-liberal orthodoxy because it takes a demand rather than a supply-side approach. The issue, I would argue, is not so much the level of state involvement, but the political purpose behind that involvement, and for whose benefit. On the one hand, as part of the IFIs "cross border initiative", it falls into the *laissez-faire* category. On the other hand, because it is an industrial policy writ regionally, it is almost a neo-Keynesian approach. "New Growth" theory, for instance, argues that active government in the economy (i.e. in physical infrastructure) can increase productivity and promote economic growth (Garrett, 1996: 80). The important point here is not only that it is difficult to label Mozal, but that regardless of its label, the politics of economic policy will determine whether it is a "partnership" for exploitation, or for development.

From a political vantage point Mozal privileges entrenched big business and an emerging elite in South Africa as well as in Mozambique. In both cases, these domestic fractions are aligned with international capital represented by the IFIs and most OECD countries. In Mozambique's case, this is troubling because it does not have the indigenous capacity to challenge IFI prescriptions. As Prakash and Hart relate, 'one expects that due to greater physical and cultural distance between transnational bureaucrats and the governed, and the lack of democratic accountability (or even accountability to the market), they (IFIs) will suffer from even greater principal-agent conflicts' (Prakash and Hart, 1999: 7). In general, it can encourage exploitation.

The "big-bang" approach that Mozal represents may bring significant GDP growth, but for it to have a wide-ranging impact on the Mozambican society one must have faith in a trickle-down effect. As stated above, the shareholders are the major constituency, and few Mozambican's are shareholders. Furthermore, as represented by the Mozal strike, capital's interest is obviously not the same as labour's interests.

With regard to the *regionalisation* of southern Africa, the impact of Mozal (and SDIs in general) is more ambiguous. Functional co-operation can be argued to promote regional co-operation and integration. However, if "politics is process", a developmental approach is losing ground to market driven integration. Corporate South Africa, particularly as represented by SACOB, disdained SADC and the developmental approach it represented. Of course, the supporters of the SDIs argue they are congruent with SADC's objectives. After all, the footer at the bottom of each page of the IDC's assessment of Mozal states, "promoting SADC development", and officials reiterate that, although bilateral, these types of project are part of regional integration/development. The partnerships are probably necessary for pushing investment into the region as during the transition South African banks were not willing to take sovereign risks in the region.[13] Eight years later this was still the case.[14] In fact, it was a challenge to get the South African banks behind the Mozal project at all (Harvard Business School, 2000: 6). But this still begs the question, who controls the process? Indeed, the SDIs are largely supported by those who originally rejected SADC. The proprietors of Mozal make no excuses for their primary responsibility to shareholders. Profits may trickle-down, but this will demand great faith in the market, and in the drivers of economic development in the region.

Notes

1. Interview with official, Mozambique Ports and Railways, Maputo, 23 May 2002.
2. Interview with Director General of Mozal, Maputo, 22 May 2002.
3. Interview with Chief, Division of Linkages, Investment Promotion Centre of Mozambique (CPI), 22 May 2002.
4. Interview with Director General of Mozal, Maputo, 22 May 2002.
5. Interview with Chief, Division of Linkages, Investment Promotion Centre of Mozambique (CPI), 22 May 2002.
6. Interview with Director General of Mozal, Maputo, 22 May 2002.
7. Discussion with Ann Edwards, a business and information systems consultant, who has evaluated customs procedures.
8. Interview with Executive Vice-President, Projects Division, IDC, Sandton, 20 May 2002.
9. Interview with Executive Vice-President, Projects Division, IDC, Sandton, 20 May 2002.
10. Interview with Director General of Mozal, Maputo, 22 May 2002.
11. Interview with Alfredo M. Guiamba, Secretary-General, National Union of Metal and Energy Workers (SINTIME), Maputo, 24 May 2002.
12. Interview with Alfredo M. Guiamba, Secretary-General, National Union of Metal and Energy Workers (SINTIME), Maputo, 25 May 2002.
13. Interview with Alister Morphet, Head, Africa Division, First Merchant Bank, Johannesburg, 1 March 1994.
14. Interview with IDC official, Sandton, 20 May 2002.

Chapter 8

A View from Maputo

Iraê Baptista-Lundin and Ian Taylor

For a state such as Mozambique, with twenty ethnicities often straddling political frontiers and bordering five countries, there exists a multiplicity of informal corridors linking the interior to the exterior. These corridors come to life in different ways. People cross borders to visit relatives or friends, they carry goods to sell or for exchange and they look for better opportunities of work or search for health care and education. During the civil war between 1976 and 1992 all neighbouring countries housed Mozambican refugees as the search for safer places impelled families to cross borders, often linking up along ethnic lines and using the route of informal corridors.

Informal corridors are a reality in Africa. One of the most vivid corridors in Mozambique, centred around Maputo, was "created" in the beginning of the 19th century when one of Shaka Zulu's generals, Shoshangane, crossed the border from South Africa during the M'fecane. Shoshangane built the Gaza Empire, one of the indigenous states in Mozambique, and he left a (new) ethnicity, the Shangaans. The reverse route of this corridor, i.e. back into South Africa, was used by the remnants of his army, who crossed back to Gazankulu when the Portuguese colonisers defeated the Gaza Empire in 1895. As a continuation of such movements, in the twentieth century the Maputo corridor has been reconstituted by South African business interests and tourists going in one direction and Mozambican migrants and informal traders going in the other direction. The question is whether the "new" Maputo corridor will be qualitatively different from the phenomena existent since pre-colonial times.

The now formalised Maputo Development Corridor (MDC) indicates a novel concept: a corridor that aims to be a factor of modernist development. Immersed in the process of regionalisation the new concept is to initiate a process of development, utilising the two states as well as the business community on both sides of the border. The series of corridors in the SADC region is also planned to formally link Mozambique with Zimbabwe, Zambia, and Malawi in order to provide transport facilities to the countries of the hinterland, using the harbours of Beira in the centre and Nacala in the north (see Tevera and Chimhowu, chapter 3). Similar projects of regionalisation are also supposed to be created involving national parks—in the process becoming trans-frontier wildlife conservation areas. One example involving Mozambique is the making of one micro-region centred on the Kruger National Park in South Africa but also linking up with parks in Mozambique and Zimbabwe to create the Great Limpopo Trans-frontier Park.

This chapter unfolds in four sections, each seeking to give a perspective drawn from commonly expressed opinions within Maputo. First, we discuss the notion held by many in Maputo that the MDC is simply a faster road for travellers and traders, and little more. Then, we examine the dynamics of the new liberalised economy within the MDC, tying this in with questions related to governance and how people in Maputo view such an important issue. It is a fact that the underlying factors that stimulated the MDC on the part of Mozambique was the need to renew national unity and reconstruct the state. Obviously, 'concerted state-building remains the necessary condition for peace building and the evolution of institutions of security and democracy' (Du Toit, 1999: 18), and in response to this concern, the analysis in this chapter discussing the difficulties of a weak state such as Mozambique in erecting such governance structures.

Connected to the above, the MDC is also analysed as a source of governance problems, creating conflicts between the government at national and local levels. Indeed, thus far the MDC has stimulated a number of contentious issues between the state and the citizens, organised in communities and interest groups. How this has played out is explored within the broader context of a complex milieu of formal and informal business/trade/service opportunities flourishing in what we may see as the "real" corridor, reinforced and accentuated by the formal MDC project and, the meta-context of neo-liberal globalisation. The current type of state in Mozambique and the form of governance that the MDC reinforces within the country are thus of crucial importance. Indeed, already the MDC has reinforced a general trend within Mozambique of seeing the "rolling back" of the state as common sense, "realistic" and pragmatic policies. Yet a discussion of the negative consequences that this has had for the state's ability to regulate economic activity and its concomitant social effects (not to mention profound fiscal implications) is vital. Finally, we sketch out some concluding thoughts. The chapter essentially seeks to understand the existence of informal corridors alongside formal African borders and how they are impacting upon the developmental trajectory of Mozambique in general, and Maputo in particular.

The MDC Through the Eyes of the People: A Faster Road

On the Mozambican side the MDC represents at present a daily crossing to South Africa for family shopping as well as for formal and informal trade and services. For many Mozambicans, this is simply "it". The wider socio-economic implications of the Corridor are poorly understood. For many Mozambicans the MDC is simply a faster and improved road facilitating trade that supplies the market in Maputo with cereal, fruits and vegetables, as well as with manufactured goods. The substantial differences in prices of goods and services between Mozambique and South Africa stimulate this intense activity. For many Mozambican traders the South African market is seen as offering the best prices for tradable goods, as well as superior quality. In general, this is something which

Mozambican producers cannot yet offer to the most affluent members of Maputo's population. For the common Mozambican then, the MDC is really a well-built and fast road. Indeed, for those struggling to build a better life, the chances offered by the Corridor *are* becoming a reality, even if they have to face difficult conditions and constantly seek to bypass the formal. Indeed, bypassing the formal procedures that supposedly exist to guide the MDC process has become the norm for many Maputo residents. A statement of a regular user indulging in *mukhero* (informal trade along the border) indicates this situation:

> None of us hold a valid passport or visa, we cross the border under the fence. We have special arrangements with some officers: "we pay and they don't see us". However, the agreement is not always respected because many times we pay and they catch us anyway. When that is so we have no choice other than either to pay again, many times with sexual services to more than one of them, or to lose our goods and risk being arrested. *Mukhero* is not an easy business, but as far as I see it at the moment it is the only alternative for us to survive.

Whilst this new road thus offers opportunities, it also offers dangers and frustrations that those involved in trading along the corridor must negotiate. According to another interviewee at the border, 'some ladies pay the boys...to enter with the goods for them. That is risky and costs money because some times they disappear, but it is the only way when the quantity of goods bought exceeds what one can carry...[T]he ladies and the boys do the risky part of the job, crossing under the fence and entering with the goods brought to the frontier by the big bosses in small pick-ups'.

Clearly, the MDC is viewed as a fast road in more ways than one in the eyes of the people: offering a window of opportunity both for the medium and small business class, and also for the poor, to make profits at both ends and along the corridor. The neighbouring city of Nelspruit constitutes an example of new opportunities offered by the MDC and is used both by the common people and by the affluent elite from Maputo and its surroundings. Located about four hours drive from Maputo, the facilities of Nelspruit are used by the elite for shopping, services, medical visits, pleasure during the week-ends, holidays and so forth. For those struggling to make a better life, the city offers a wide range of business opportunities, particularly as the price differences between the two countries constitute a chance not to be missed, especially when payment of duties can be "negotiated".

Opportunities are there to be grasped then, even if life is not easy. All social groups in Mozambique complain that crossing the formal border constitutes a constant headache, because there are no fixed rules and everything is up for negotiation. This situation of course contrasts with the commonly held assumption that the MDC has cut down on corruption and predatory activities by state actors. On the contrary, some Maputo residents argue that the reverse has occurred. This is true both for the formal and the "informal" payment of duties. One interviewee claimed that 'the amount of money paid today may increase dramatically tomorrow. There is always a need to bargain and take chances'.

Witbank at the South African end of the MDC is seldom used by the common Mozambican. The neighbourhood and cities of Mapalane, Komatipoort and Nelspruit are the places offering special arrangements in terms of business opportunities, thus prematurely shortening the MDC for many Maputo people. They are not interested in some Maputo-Witbank road, however renovated it may be. What they see and use is the faster link between their Mozambican locales and the trading opportunities perceived to exist in nearby Nelspruit and other Mpumalanga towns.

The "New Economy" and the Market Dynamics of the MDCs

During the time of the centrally planned economy, cities in Mozambique such as Maputo functioned under a system of rationing cards for food and fuel. Specific stores and co-operatives took care of the supply and the distribution of goods. All services were under the central control of the state, including the system of transport and import-exports and all but a few people worked for the Mozambican state.

However, it was gradually realised that the centrally planned economy could not sufficiently deliver what it was supposed to do in order to satisfy the needs of the citizenry. This was for a myriad of reasons, most notably a lack of experience in government management and the shortage of qualified people, mismanagement and, of course, internal and external sabotage. The armed conflict launched in 1976, which destroyed a huge amount of infrastructure, made it much more difficult to transport goods and greatly hampered the Frelimo state in its attempts at constructing its own form of Afro-socialism. In 1984, after more than a decade of central planning, Mozambique started to change its economic policy. This process led to the acceptance of the conditions demanded by the international financial institutions (IFIs), and in January 1987 Mozambique adopted a structural adjustment programme. These emergency measures were introduced with the aim of changing the course of the economy through a radical liberalisation project. The bulk of such policies continue today, effectively marking a retreat from the government's original commandist position and exemplifying the degree to which Frelimo has shed its socialist pretensions.

It is within this market driven context that the MDC functions. Today, all transactions are regulated by so-called "market principles". For some, this has been of benefit, even whilst the majority of Maputo's residents face further marginalisation. Amongst the beneficiaries have been those who indulged in (illegal) market activities even when Mozambique was ostensibly "socialist". They have emerged from the shadows during the current dispensation to enrich themselves through a continuation of various schemes and activities. Their roots lie in the period when Frelimo was experimenting with a socialist-informed economy. Illegal commercial activity—known as the *candonga*—appeared, especially in the urban areas. Under the *candonga* goods and services were bought or provided parallel to the controlled prices. Although illegal, punished by the state and condemned by civil society as economic sabotage, the *candonga* existed throughout the socialist period. The money accumulated by these means at the time of scarcity is now used to invest in legal operations. Indeed, the window opened to the private sector since 1987 has given a chance to many individuals to make a life out of business, including the former *candongueiros*. Many of these characters are at present frequent users of the rebuilt road to South Africa, constituting what can be called a (new) social class of people in small business. For many of these it is a continuation of opportunities that have been in operation for quite a while whilst for others it constitutes a new opportunity to join the ranks of those made rich as *candongueiros*.

There is however, another side to this "reality of plenty" as some call it. The formal and informal business activity associated with the Corridor *are* providing a better living for many, this cannot be disputed, but at the same time much of the economic activities currently being pursued is simply one-way traffic i.e. the importation of cheap goods from South Africa to be re-sold in Mozambique. This has the effect of preventing the recovery of the productive sector in Mozambique, which has still not really recovered after sixteen years of armed conflict. Thus whilst entrepreneurs get rich selling cheap imported goods, utilising the new road as a speedy conduit, they prevent their own country from industrialising and recovering. At the same time, goods imported into Mozambique are entering the country almost always without the payment of duties, largely due to corrupt "arrangements" between the entrepreneurs and the border customs. This not only harms the state through loss of revenue, but also represents further unfair competition to local industry, which sees its competitive edge lost to cheap goods flooding the streets of Maputo. This is creating a situation where Mozambique is becoming a country of consumers of products and services manufactured and provided by South Africa. This may be good for the consumer in the short-term but long-term prospects for Mozambique escaping its position of over-weaning dependence upon South Africa erode by the day. This leads us to argue that the "sustainability" of Mozambican development is under great threat due to processes unlocked by the liberalisation movement stemming from the 1980s *and* the overall opportunities facilitated by the MDC in an environment where capacity (or willingness, due to corruption) to monitor commercial activity is weak.

In addition, the security of the borders is of concern not only because of smuggling commercial goods but also because of the traffic in drugs, small arms and cash. Estimates of weapons imported into Mozambique during the civil war range from 500,000 to six million. During the United Nations peacekeeping operation of 1993-95, about 190,000 weapons were collected. However, most weapons were not destroyed and through various corrupt practices they were soon back in the public domain, either circulating within Mozambique or being sold and illegally smuggled into neighbouring states, the main destination being South Africa. In four recovery operations performed jointly by South African and Mozambican authorities in recent years, a total of 11,891 firearms were seized and destroyed. These have included over 100 pistols, 6,000 anti-personnel mines, and hundreds of the ubiquitous AK-47. Also captured were over three million rounds of ammunition (*Business Day*, Johannesburg, 18 January 2000).

Such a profusion of illegal weaponry flows back and forth along the micro-region, much of it for hire at hourly rates. This criminality surely erodes any coherent notion of a security community, at least at the ground level and, lofty rhetoric aside, there has been a lack of success in stopping such illegal activity within the micro-region. In fact, recently it was announced that there exist 144 organised criminal syndicates specialising in offences ranging from cash heists to stock theft operating in Mpumalanga, many with strong links to criminals in Mozambique. These syndicates also act as conduits for drug smugglers along the Gauteng-Maputo nexus, using their organisations for drug and weapon smuggling, counterfeiting money, cross-border vehicle smuggling and (increasingly) subverting government through corruption (*Business Day*, 28 March 2000). Though it is not covered in any MDC prospectus, the "real" micro-region is made up of a host of hubs and spokes of illicit activities, a large degree of which are historically long-standing. Indeed, given the apartheid regime's covert support of anti-government bandits during the destabilisation campaign against Frelimo, the "returning home" in the hands of criminals of much of the weaponry provided by Pretoria to Renamo is grimly ironic.

Returning to the trade issue, for national producers, it is important to highlight the question of high local taxes charged compared to the "free profits" of the informal traders, which easily escape fiscal control. These factors are important because they discourage those operating within the law and in fact may well stimulate a turn to criminal activities. The informal commerce in agricultural products such as tomatoes, potatoes and onions has almost destroyed local Mozambican businesses in these products and frozen chickens from South Africa are sold cheaper than those produced by the Unions of Co-operatives established in the Green Zones of Maputo. Importantly, most producers of the aforementioned produce are women and many of them are heads of households. The collapse of the cashew industry is one of the most striking examples of a bad customs policy adopted under the guidance of the IFIs whilst the sugar industry is also in a dangerous situation because of systematic smuggling. Other smaller industries such as cooking oil, soap and hygienic articles are also in difficult situations. In all, in many cases the MDC has turned out to be a factor of maldevelopment for many Mozambicans and if producers in Mozambique abide by the rules and regulations that supposedly govern the formal corridor they will simply go out of business, sooner rather than later.

As a means of responding to such actualities and to try and contain the apparent negative effects of the MDC on local producers, there is a move to review fiscal policy as a whole in Mozambique, specifically to lower value added taxes. Such moves indicate that the politicians in Maputo *are* aware that the open market policy of the MDC constitutes a problem for local producers. However, the ability to implement such defensive measures are immediately undermined by the low level of political governance demanded by both the IFIs (as part of the neo-liberal restructuring of the Mozambican state) and, by the overall scepticism towards state involvement inherent in the SDI paradigm. Indeed, the negative effects of the sudden opening up of Mozambique's markets have been worsened—if not created—by the state's inability to prevent the practice of smuggling and its failure to "catch" the informal importers and thus receive payment of duties. It seems that in Maputo opportunities for one section of the community, facilitated by the MDC, represent loss to others, be they local producers or the wider state. This occurs within the broader context where the capacity of the state to manage such impulses (already weak due to historical reasons) has been further eroded by the anti-state logic of neo-liberalism.

The Issue of Governance in Mozambique

It is vital to ask whether the goals expressed by the MDC project are shared and owned by the majority in Maputo. This is particularly so in a country with a high level of dependency on external aid and where investments mostly come from an overwhelmingly strong (in regional terms) state such as South Africa. The question of political governance and ownership is crucial, particularly within the context of a country beset by widespread poverty and social dislocation. Such a situation requires state institutions that are strong and functional enough to protect national interests and care for the population in terms of providing services and human security. Under neo-liberalism, which underpins both contemporary globalisation and the developmental philosophy of the MDC SDI, the maxim is a minimal state.

This minimalist state undermines the expectations on the part of Mozambicans that their newly democratised state will be more accountable and transparent in its regulatory actions, delivering better services and interacting with civil society in an active and participatory dialogue has not yet been fulfilled. It is a fact that the MDC has failed to increase the ability of the Mozambican state to establish dialogue on equal terms with the international community. Regarding political governance, very little has improved so far and the ability of the government to raise its voice when dealing with international capital is as low as before: the quality and type of governance that is emerging and being consolidated in Mozambique is rather questionable, to say the least. Indeed, Maputo's capacity may actually be lower now when or since it has to operate within the constraints of surveillance by neo-liberal watchdogs, such as the IFIs and many of the donors. Certainly, the latitude of the government to make an independent plan of development is narrow, if existent at all and this is exacerbated by the strategy within the MDC which demands a retreat of the state and a fundamental change in the ownership of the economy facilitated through privatisation and liberalisation.

This whole process has been propitiated by a seeming policy "fit" between the ANC's GEAR project and Frelimo's neo-liberal conversion. As we have mentioned, the Mozambican state elites have been (at times reluctantly) pursuing a neo-liberal project since they implemented an Economic Recovery Programme in 1987, largely at the behest of disciplinary agents such as the World Bank, the IMF and other "donors", who supply the bulk of Mozambique's income. This has been spurred on by the paucity of alternative visions amongst Frelimo regarding recovery strategies. Maputo's approach is very much in line with the norms demanded by international capital and appealing to the need to positively engage in the globalisation process, signalling the tailing off, if not the closure, of Frelimo's progressive project embarked upon from the mid-1970s onwards: Frelimo's historic retreat to capitalism. Not that this has brought much reward for the average Mozambican: after twelve years of economic reforms 70 per cent of the population still live in absolute poverty (*South African Press Agency*, Pretoria, 25 February 1999).

Political governance—as an act in delivering to constituents what is expected in terms of services and security—is thus highly constrained within the MDC. This is the current reality within regional projects such as the MDC, where the participation of the citizens if/when invoked, takes place more in the form of information and less with regard to participatory consultations. This being so, the space for good political governance is diluted under a low level of popular sovereignty that is extremely narrow. This is the case of Mozambique, with an infant democracy and feeble state institutions and where seventy per cent of the population live below the absolute poverty line. Such a picture offers of course almost no room for real sovereignty. Yet it seems obvious that real sovereignty seems to be a precondition for genuine regionalism and balanced, rather than uneven regional development. The framework currently offered by the MDC provides a window of opportunity for those within the state and those citizens in positions to serve the interest of big capital or, at a low but growing level, those who may profit privately in trading networks as a means of accumulation. This framework however can only offer uneven development: between the rural and urban; between Maputo and the rest of Mozambique; between different classes within Maputo; and of course, between Mozambique and South Africa.

Concluding Reflections: Who is Really Benefiting From the MDC?

It is true that the MDC is bringing about changes in Mozambique, providing infrastructures both in terms of the new road and of the industrial plants constructed so far and, as we have mentioned, opening up opportunities to some elements of society in Maputo. The *quality* or appropriateness of what is provided is generally not questioned because such concerns are obfuscated by the country's needs. In the current milieu, it seems all or any investment is welcome and negative consequences are brushed over or ignored. However, our analytical reading of the MDC reflects a situation that if not revisited could cause more harm than good. To make the Maputo Corridor a successful project in the region, not only in the eyes of the state in macro-economic terms but also of the common Mozambican, it is necessary to increase not only the level of political governance but also economic governance in Mozambique. An active participation and vigilant stance by the state would be a good start.

Considering the above, a final reflection is summarised from two angles: the formal corridor, i.e. the MDC as a conduit for the Mozambican state and the business community; and the corridor for the common people. The official MDC is meant to be a facilitator of development. However, there are problems that have so far not been solved satisfactorily, provoking important questions as to who is really benefiting from the formal project? Any answer to this question must be multidimensional. As a faster road, the MDC provides an opportunity for trade, though the creation of an informal business class threatens, as we have seen, local agriculture and industry. A small elite or *comprador* group is being created, building a new economic class but without any organic link to a productive sector in Mozambique. Thus it remains open to question whether there is any real potentiality for the MDC to contribute to building sustainable development when local industry around Maputo is suffering from the massive import of manufactured goods and national agriculture is suffocated by cheap food imported without proper regulations.

In macro-economic terms the MDC has already produced what could be called, the "Mozal effect" on the local economy. During the presentation of the annual state of the nation address to parliament at the end of 2001, the cabinet used two figures for revenues: one including Mozal and another one without. The plant is thus "distorting" the economy in macro-economic terms. Whether it is good or bad is an open question to be discussed at two levels: on macro-economic terms on the one hand; and on the issue of dependency versus sovereignty on the other. In the context of a dependant relationship that currently exists between Mozambique and South Africa, figures representing macro-economic improvement invariably reflect growth rather than development—an important distinction often missed by the more enthusiastic commentators on Mozambique's post-war "miracle". Indeed, what *type* of development being reinforced by the MDC is a serious question. Is it sustainable grass-roots development with the potential for future evolution and expansion, or is it, at the local level short-term in nature, oriented to the quick accumulation of capital, but at the expense of local production and the long-term well-being of Mozambique? At the "highest" level, is the development being generated simply centred around the mega-projects, with little lasting organic links to the host country, other than increased receipts in terms of capital flows?

The whole idea of a formalised corridor as a factor of development resembles a double-edged sword cutting on both sides. The positive side of the MDC is reflected in macro-economic terms: increasing GNP and national income in general terms. The negative side is reflected in the destruction of Mozambique's productive sectors and in the low level of governance in the country, which the MDC has made very little contribution to. Indeed, by its active embrace of essentially neo-liberal prescriptions for promoting development, this situation may very well get worse. To find a balance between the possibilities and the risks engendered by the MDC constitutes a major task for all stakeholders in the project. The satisfactory resolution of these conundrums will determine the judgement passed on the formal MDC by the Mozambican people themselves. Such a situation provides a major challenge to the architects and promoters of the Maputo Development Corridor.

Chapter 9

Conclusion

Fredrik Söderbaum and Ian Taylor

Micro-regions are emerging all over the world, not least in southern Africa where "real"/informal micro-regional spaces are being utilised by both the state and the private sector as building blocks upon which "development corridors" can be constructed as a means to promote growth and development. With regard to this relatively new development, the SDIs are the most interesting of the policy-driven type of micro-regionalism in southern Africa, and the Maputo Development Corridor (MDC) has been publicly advanced and promoted as the "flagship" of these SDIs. In consequence it may be argued that the MDC constitutes perhaps the most important contemporary case of micro-regionalism in southern Africa.

Most research found under the banner of regionalism studies (at least in the field of IPE) has tended to treat the micro-regional phenomenon in a largely superficial manner. By engaging regional processes on the micro-level and "on the ground" in the MDC, this volume has sought to advance our understanding of how southern Africa and its communities are currently being reconfigured. The aim of this study has been to examine the MDC with a strategic focus on governance and development, addressing such key questions as who decides what and with what means in the MDC (i.e. the governance factor). This then ties in with the second focus, namely who is benefiting from the MDC and who is being excluded and in what way (i.e. the development factor). This particular focus follows directly from the ambition to build upon and advance the new regionalism approach (NRA).

The NRA seeks to avoid the exaggerated state-centrism inherent in much of mainstream theorising in the field and critically assesses state-society complexes as well as the formal/informal dimensions in the formation of regions. The state is clearly not the only regionalising actor, and a variety of non-state market and society actors are involved in the construction and reconstruction of regions. As the MDC shows, the state cannot be taken for granted, and sometimes the state may even have a negative impact on both governance and development. With this said, however, the state should not and cannot be wished away. The state is thus both part of the problem and the solution for questions of governance and development.

What differentiates the NRA and this volume from much of the mainstream literature in the field of regionalism is that both seek to transcend a narrow focus on the "formal" project and policy-making as such. In so doing this volume has paid particular attention to more "informal" processes and how local communities regard and respond to the MDC initiative "on the ground". The impact of the MDC on local communities is crucial in attempting to come to conclusions regarding governance and development along the corridor. Currently, superficial analyses of Mozambique hold it up to be some sort of "miracle". With its high economic growth rate (around 11 per cent), relatively stable currency and low inflation (2.5 per cent), from a narrow economistic stance, Mozambique seems to be "going places" and the MDC is often invoked as an important component of this "miraculous" trajectory. However, deeper studies—of which this book has tried to contribute to—reveal a country and a micro-region that is not as healthy as the economists and the official rhetoric would like us to believe. Indeed, the benefits of this high growth rate remain largely elusive for both the urban working class and the rural peasantry. The current statutory minimum wage in industry is only about US$37 per month, less than half the basic needs of a worker and his/her dependants. In addition, large segments of the population within the micro-region remain marginalised and excluded.

This final chapter draws theoretical and empirical conclusions, especially with regard to the two key focus areas of the volume: governance and development. The analysis is divided into three sections. The first section concentrates on governance. One crucial feature of the NRA approach is to unpack the state-society complex and understand the changing nature of the state in the context of globalisation and various forms of regionalisation. This is particularly so as globalisation implies the reorganisation and the restructuring of the state as well as constructing new patterns of inclusion and exclusion. This is quite apparent in the case of the MDC, which is an instrument to reorganise the state and has brought about a restructuring of governance within the micro-region, with profound implications for both the Mozambican and South African national governments and their citizens.

Development is considered in the second section. This volume has shown that the MDC is specifically designed to "bring" globalisation and crowd in global capital to southern Africa. In so doing, policy-makers have adopted a particular stance, according to which development is defined and pursued within a neo-liberal framework and seems to be narrowly predicated around "growth". The section draws conclusions with regard to what type of development is being facilitated by the MDC, and for whom and for what purpose. The chapter concludes with a consideration of the future of micro-regionalism in southern Africa. While it is acknowledged that the MDC does contain some positive features, these aspects are largely eclipsed by the negatives. The uneven development impulses reinforced by the MDC and the ineffectiveness of its governance radically undermine the potentiality of the MDC as a "model" SDI for the rest of the southern African region. We are sceptical that such a spatially focused framework engineered, in the main, by the private sector can stimulate genuine long-term and sustainable development. In a region characterised by a labour surplus (albeit largely unskilled), highly capital intensive and "big-bang" development projects do not seem particularly apposite. Essentially, we conclude that a private sector driven model, which is supposed to replace (or even by-pass) the state is questionable if broad-based development, which after all is what the MDC prospectus claims the initiative is all about, is to be advanced.

The MDC and Governance

As repeatedly pointed out in this volume, the development paradigm of the MDC is closely associated with the hegemonic discourse of neo-liberalism and the concomitant ambition to tie into and reinforce processes associated with economic globalisation. This has now been fairly long-standing in the region. Micro-regionalism, as it is being pursued in the form of the MDC, is best understood as one instrument in such a broader strategy. The same rationale is stressed by the current South African President, Thabo Mbeki, who has pronounced that SDIs and development corridors contribute to the 'African renaissance' at the same time as they 'bring' globalisation to Africa (DBSA, 2001a). This draws attention to the fact that policy-makers view the MDC and the SDIs as "fitting" economic globalisation and that they advance continental regionalism as well as other forms of macro-regional economic integration and co-operation. Here it must be underlined that the MDC is also designed to be compatible with both South Africa's and Mozambique's national economic reform programmes and the notion of "good governance". In effect, the prevailing paradigm, which the MDC is founded upon, contains a very strong emphasis on the notion that the state is inefficient and needs to be deregulated and made more competent. According to this view, state intervention is seen as a distortion, whereas the (global) "market" is seen as the solution and engine of growth, allocating resources more reasonably than the state.

This is not to say that the state is seen as totally redundant. As has been shown, the state is often rather pro-active in the MDC, albeit largely in the realms of promoting new investments, the negotiation of public-private partnerships (PPPs) and the facilitation of an enabling environment for "the market" to operate in. The state's governance role is thus transformed by the SDI model in an intriguing way: rolled back *vis-à-vis* social progress but pro-active in encouraging economic growth and bankable private investment (narrowly defined). It is this reconfigured posture that confirms that the MDC has seen the state in both Mozambique and South Africa reduced to what can be seen as a transmission belt for capital, neglecting in the main questions pertaining to social and participatory development. As we (Söderbaum and Taylor) argue in chapter 4, one of the main roles of the state is to act as a giant investment promotion agency, in order to crowd in foreign capital. In other words, what this neo-liberal paradigm does not encourage (or even allow in many respects) is a role for the state to advance participation, democracy, social development and equity in any meaningful way.

Baptista-Lundin and Taylor (chapter 8) clearly demonstrate that in Mozambique expectations that the post-civil war state would be more accountable and deliver better services has been largely disappointed. Even a supposedly strengthened peacetime Mozambican state has, through the adoption of neo-liberal prescriptions, been found wanting in its ability to formulate any strong voice regarding its interactions with the international community. Certainly, the latitude of the government to make an independent plan of governance/development is narrow and is under incessant interrogation by the disciplinary watchdogs of international capitalism, something which also South Africa, operating its own self-imposed structural adjustment programme (i.e. GEAR) has been largely unable to avoid (Taylor, 2001).

However, as Hentz correctly points out in chapter 7, the key to any discussion of these issues is not so much the level of state involvement in the economy as such, but the *political purpose* behind that involvement. Building on general insights from critical international political economy (including the NRA), many of the chapters in this volume draw attention to the reality that the political purpose behind the state's involvement has not been to promote development and public goods or needs, but has rather been first and foremost to promote an enabling environment for the private sector. The privatisation of state assets and the formation of various forms of "partnerships" goes hand in hand with such impulses (Söderbaum and Taylor, chapter 4; Söderbaum, chapter 5; Ngwenya and Taylor, chapter 6; Hentz, chapter 7). Undoubtedly this is both a political (governance) and an economic (development) strategy; the two are inseparable. In the case of the MDC, this strategy is being demonstrated when the state has difficulty raising funds for investment in infrastructure (which was previously considered a core state function). The new solution is now to find "alternative" sources of funding, ranging from outright privatisation to various kinds of PPPs. Within the MDC the most comprehensive PPPs are the Witbank-Maputo N4 toll road (Ngwenya and Taylor, chapter 6), the Ressano Garcia/Nkomati border post and the Maputo port, with the Mozal being one particular kind of partnership between the public and the private sector (Hentz, chapter 7). What this has meant is that in the MDC both private and public actors are building and operating many of the infrastructural projects in the region. Here it is crucial to recognise that such activity is on a strictly commercial basis and in accepting this approach to governance, development and infrastructure, the state has become the disciplining spokesman of global economic forces. As we argue in chapter 4, the classical task of nation-building and public governance has been radically transformed. What is normally considered a public good (in this case a road) is turned into a semi-private good.

It is important to recognise that this does not suggest that the state is simply "disappearing". What it suggests is, as Baptista-Lundin and Taylor (chapter 8) point out, that a small elite or *comprador* group is constructing and benefiting from the MDC, and that this elite class has very little organic links to the productive sectors. Hentz (chapter 7) shares this scepticism, arguing that in the case of Mozal, entrenched big business (largely South African) and an emerging politico-economic elite (in both Mozambique and South Africa) are more and more privileged at the expense of the "average" person. This is likely to be exacerbated as the domestic elite factions are aligned with and bolstered by international capital. This conclusion is in line with critical IPE studies of regionalism elsewhere, which often remain sceptical of much of the "really existing regionalism" and the underlying motives of the leading actors. For instance, as argued by Kearns and Hook, 'regionalism is fundamentally an elite-led process wherever one looks around the world and, indeed...it is often used in its own right to out-manoeuvre and stifle popular opposition to the kind of politics and neo-liberal economy which it itself represents' (Kearns and Hook, 1999: 249-50).

From this volume's analysis, it is thus clear that the governance structures and the PPPs operating in the MDC have had a mainly negative effect on governance, democracy, ownership and participation. The NRA suggests that this simply reflects the hegemony of neo-liberalism in the current era, emphasising low public expenditure, deficit reduction and extolling (almost at all cost) a low national debt. As part of this broader project, the call for "partnerships" usually involves the commercialisation of state activity, often leading to outright privatisation. The problem with this strategy is that the commercial viability of a project is the main criteria for a PPP. In essence, profit comes before people and issues such as social inclusion. In societies such as Mozambique and South Africa, with an abundance of market failures, gross inequalities and suffering from traumatic pasts, it is questionable whether such a profit-minded framework is the best foundation for promoting participation, governance and development in a post-apartheid southern Africa. As Ngwenya and Taylor (chapter 6) assert, it would be a mistake if the PPP "philosophy" was taken on board as the new "one-size-fits-all" panacea for facilitating Africa's governance and development. Whilst the PPP approach may offer *partial* solutions to promoting growth and *some* limited development in the micro-region, a more careful appraisal of the pitfalls that such a model engenders clearly needs to be thought through, if the experience of the MDC is anything to go by. Moreover, Söderbaum (chapter 5) argues that the particular mode of governance in the MDC is designed in order to handle relationships between the state and mostly foreign business rather than ensure participation for people living in the corridor area. The point is that the informal and almost "hidden" mode of governance in the MDC works relatively well for those included in the governance structure while it excludes those on the "outside".

The (In)Effectiveness of Governance

With regard to the more specific governance issues, the MDC has thrown up a welter of evidence that national and provincial governments need to maintain a very regular dialogue if something like an MDC-inspired SDI is to succeed elsewhere. This volume brings attention to the importance of political commitment and political leadership for the success or failure of a micro-regional initiative. In the MDC, the political champions proved to be very important, and their commitment and devotion to the project was crucial in getting the project going and also maintaining its momentum during the initial phases. However, at the same time these processes made the MDC very vulnerable as when political mismanagement and political interest in the MDC deteriorated the whole project received a major blow (De Beer and Arkwright, chapter 2; Söderbaum, chapter 5; Ngwenya and Taylor, chapter 6). As a matter of fact, the political support provided by the "political champions" and the specially designed SDI methodology has not worked satisfactorily. The important thing here is that despite concerns expressed by the private sector to government to take the MDC initiative more seriously, the MDC has increasingly become characterised by a lack of political leadership (either nationally or provincially in South Africa). A noticeable decline in functioning governance structures within the MDC has simultaneously occurred. Although the MDC is basically informed by a neo-liberal "hands-off" approach to governance/development, it does not and should not totally emasculate the state from any involvement. In fact, the strategy vitally needs a supportive environment at the policy level, through plans and strategies, in order for it to succeed.

Yet, the MDC has failed to maintain a functioning relationship between national and provincial levels of government. As demonstrated by De Beer and Arkwright (chapter 2), the admixture of a very centralised and dominant approach from national government (in the case of South Africa anyway), combined with important changes at a political and official level in Mpumalanga since the end of 1999, have brought about a situation where the administration in Mpumalanga has not been able to effectively take on the broader development planning and project programming processes inherent in the MDC project. Indeed, De Beer and Arkwright note that the MDC initiative has in the South African context (and probably even in the Mozambique context, though to a lesser degree) become increasingly marked by some of the "bottlenecks" that the SDI methodology was originally designed to avoid. They go on to argue that it seems clear that unless the MDC initiative receives some urgent political support and priority to raise its profile and performance, there appears to be a very good chance that the MDC will slowly fade into oblivion, with immense implications for other envisioned SDIs.

Söderbaum (chapter 5) also draws attention to the situation at the national-provincial relation, which has thus far constituted a weak link in the governance of the MDC. Co-operation between central government and the province started out reasonably well, but gradually the MDC project was centralised rather than decentralised. A top-down and centralised strategy may work at the central government level, but it tends to be ineffective on the ground as well as being met with local resistance, something which a number of the chapters in this volume have highlighted. The handing over and "exit strategy" has clearly not worked very well, something that needs to be accommodated and rethought for future regional SDIs. Having said that, as Söderbaum points out, there are certain strengths with the networked institutional structure within the MDC. Ensuring a quick and flexible planning and decision-making process is one of these. But it is most doubtful whether such a fluid and loosely organised network structure and its associated fast-track approach is suitable for the existing bureaucratic and institutional realities in southern Africa. This is particularly when it is apparent that the governance structure does not seem to work when institutional capacities are weak, as they are in many parts of the region. The implications of the governance problems identified above for developmental issues in the MDC is what we turn to next.

The MDC and (Uneven) Development

There are several methodological difficulties in assessing the "development" impact of the MDC. For instance, because of its recent origin it is difficult to examine the developmental impact of the MDC in separation from the broader economy. However, this does not mean that any analysis of the developmental implications of the MDC is impossible. As this volume has shown, much can be said. As a start, many chapters in this volume emphasise that there is a discrepancy between the objectives of the MDC and the "actually existing" MDC. On paper the aims and objectives of the MDC are rather impressive. However, there is a wide rift between rhetoric and practical implementation; between the emphasis placed on bankable and "big-bang" investment projects, on the one hand, and social development, job creation and a participatory and holistic development strategy, on the other. The emphasis placed on bankable investment projects is out of proportion compared to the minor spending that is spent on MDC key objectives 3 and 4, which are supposed to deal with "development" (see De Beer and Arkwright, chapter 2; Tevera and Chimhowu, chapter 3; Söderbaum and Taylor, chapter 4). For sure, the MDC is officially held to be a development corridor, but in practice it is an investment and "market guidance" initiative with the hope that it will create jobs and somehow lead to "development". Therefore, there is a contradiction in the content of the MDC, which is obviously a weakness and undermines the credibility and functioning of the project. In fact, certain leading government officials behind the MDC admit that the MDC is not about development at all: it is to be understood as the Maputo *Investment* Corridor. Furthermore, the fact of the matter is that there exists no compelling evidence that the implementation of capital-intensive "mega-projects", the cornerstone of the MDC, have a particularly positive impact on development as such, particularly not under conditions such as those prevailing in Mpumalanga and Mozambique.

Indeed, as discussed in several chapters, one serious weakness in the "development" paradigm of the MDC is the misplaced belief that large-scale ("big-bang") investment projects will automatically create upstream/downstream and horizontal linkages. Such strategies manifestly fail to generate large numbers of low cost employment opportunities. In a micro-region where unemployment is at almost chronic levels this is a very serious problem. Obviously, as Hentz (chapter 7) shows, some jobs are of course created by such projects. However, much of these are temporary, created during the initial construction phase and are of a low-skilled variety with very little skills transfer. After the construction of such projects, the bulk of the formerly employed are largely redundant, whilst skilled workers (invariably outsiders in the context of the MDC) take up positions. This then leaves a project appearing in isolation from the broader surrounding community, with all the negative perceptions and consequences that this may engender, particularly if we are discussing the developmental aspects of the MDC. Weaknesses related to the financial and technical capacity constraints experienced by the Mpumalanga government have also negatively impacted upon the developmental potential of the MDC. It seems clear that the negative features of the governance mechanisms (see above), in combination with the development paradigm (no spending on social development and a naïve trust in trickle-down) is a bad combination, together reinforcing one another negatively.

MDC as an Image

A sceptical view may assert that the MDC should be seen as, in part, simply an image-boosting exercise for the assorted elites in Mozambique and South Africa. There are several indications that this is part of the story. It is astonishing how rapidly SDIs and development corridors have become such a widespread and influential feature in southern Africa and have been elevated to the status of a cure-all model for the region. Yet whether this is all simply hype is an important question to answer: the material dimension of the MDC is deeply intertwined with discursive and ideational variables. For instance, the axis between Johannesburg and Maputo has been a "corridor" for more than hundred years, but today the official view is that it should now be seen as a "development corridor". What several of the chapters in this volume suggest is that the region-builders behind the MDC have sought to create a panoply of positive images of the MDC, simply by making unwarranted associations with the Asian growth model and by merely labelling it a "development corridor".

As a project, the MDC is created by a small number of political and economic entrepreneurs and policy-makers, grouped together in an epistemic community. These entrepreneurs have (rather successfully) managed to create an image that the involved governments and provinces are fostering development, economic growth and regional economic integration, while in reality the main thrust of the MDC is to facilitate private mega-projects and to enhance and broaden the ongoing process of privatising the state. In a similar fashion, the privatisation of the N4 toll road between Witbank and Maputo was packaged (or "masked") as part of a broader growth project. Without this façade the negative consequences for the poor would be much more evident and the legitimacy of the whole MDC project would be radically undermined. In this sense the "development" components of the MDC are social and cognitive rather than simply a material construction and, at least to some extent, it can even be seen as an illusionary construction. In short, just because regional elites proclaim the MDC to be a "development corridor" does not make it so.

Yet another example of this trend is that one of the primary motives of the MDC was to "show the world" that Mozambique could handle gigantic initiatives, such as the Mozal and the toll road. The importance of this can hardly be exaggerated, and when seen in this perspective human development was only of secondary importance. In fact, the demonstration effect that the MDC has sought to perform—at least at a rhetorical level—feeds into the whole post-war Mozambican "miracle" myth and is extremely powerful. What this book in part has sought to do is to strip away such rhetoric and rather analyse the concrete manifestations of this supposed "miracle" within the context of the MDC.

The Future of Micro-regionalism in Southern Africa

The MDC is likely to remain one of the most well known and recognised micro-regions in (southern) Africa, although its future is not altogether certain. One future scenario is the strengthening of the neo-liberal project which seems to result in uneven development and the fragmentation of the "real"/informal micro-region. This implies a continuation of the present trend whereby the corridor is designed mainly for large-scale capital and exporters in the formal economy. In a more positive scenario, however, there is a potential for the consolidation of the MDC in a more developmental sense, whereby the informal "real" corridor and the formal MDC project can become mutually reinforcing. The development strategy of the formal micro-region *can* be redesigned to promote the welfare and needs of the people inhabiting the area, and the governance mechanisms *can* be strengthened to enhance this project.

Yet, this book has been largely critical of the developmental impulses (or lack of them) that seem to characterise the MDC and many of our conclusions are not very positive. The "market" cannot be left to its own devices if development and empowerment within the MDC (and indeed other SDIs) is to be realised. This is particularly so if much of the private sector investing in the various projects are White South African-owned, whose developmental vision in engaging in the MDC is open to serious interrogation. Certainly, the sense of social responsibility of South African business remains generally very low. Rather, forms of participatory development offer a means by which the developmental initiatives of the MDC can be guided and, crucially, evaluated. If this is not so, alienation and exclusion can quickly act as counterforces to any positive attributes emanating from the ostensible developmental projects. (Re)capturing a truly development- and people-centred regional project within the MDC initiative must therefore remain fundamental to the rebuilding of the MDC and other similar projects in Africa. This can only occur if the top-down tendencies thus exhibited by the MDC are married to bottom-up initiatives centred around accountability, democracy and social upliftment. This upliftment must have the interests of the marginalised populations within the micro-region at its heart. It is not good enough to predicate the micro-region simply around "growth" and "big-bang" investment, and then simply *hope* that "trickle-down", job creation and empowerment will occur. As Turok remarked, 'the pursuit of economic growth without the simultaneous pursuit of development will lead to a dead end' (quoted in *Mail and Guardian*, Johannesburg, 2-8 July, 1999).

It should be remarked that the MDC does, however, contain several novel and positive features and the problematic aspects can be overcome through some strategic changes in the MDC approach, such as a heavier focus on "development", and more comprehensive and inclusive governance structures. Only if such fundamental problems are concretely and actively addressed can the impulses currently animating the micro-region be deployed in the service of those who most need them. Whether this is possible in an epoch where neo-liberalism is currently hegemonic amongst the elite classes, provides those with a more compassionate vision for the MDC with their greatest challenge. Following on from this, it seems clear that the extent to which the MDC is replicable elsewhere in the southern African region is questionable and needs careful consideration. Clearly, both historical and geographical factors provided a unique setting for the MDC which is difficult to replicate elsewhere in the SADC region. In other words, using the MDC approach elsewhere in southern Africa may, just like in the case of the MDC itself, lead to exaggerated negative effects in terms of uneven development, as well as exclusion. It is thus very unclear whether the spatially focused approach, driven by private investment, will be able to trigger genuine "development" in the targeted areas. Indeed, the SDI strategy is a highly capital intensive development strategy that may not be suitable for regional economies whose main endowments are labour and natural raw resources. It is certainly difficult to expect that internal and external capital will start investing in lagging areas just because they have been officially declared "development zones", "development corridors" etc. This returns us to our critique of the discursive nature of much of the MDC project.

The rolling back of the state and the new forms of (neo-liberal) governance/development are obviously intended to give private agents a greater role in the economy and change the ownership base of the economy. In official rhetoric this strategy is assumed to serve the public interest, often wrapped up in notions of "partnerships" (see Ngwenya and Taylor, chapter, 6; Hentz, chapter 7). However, critical IPE and the NRA draws attention to the reality that the resulting political economy and any accrued development is much less than what it pretends to be. Even the most energetic advocates of this discourse, such as the IMF and the World Bank, are now starting to accept that "trickle-down" does not work in the absence of functioning political authority and governance. But what many proponents continue to neglect is the fact that the image of an "open" and "liberalised" market hides the real power relations and structural imbalances of this market. The resulting regionalism we are witnessing is therefore utterly "thin" and exclusionist, constructed by powerful political elite and capitalist interests (from within as well as outside the region) with little concern for human development. In fact, this type of regionalism is unable to accommodate the interests of the poor, disadvantaged and unemployed, who lack any means to participate and much less so to "compete" on the global market. In short we assert that neo-liberal regionalism in southern Africa uses the public face of international and regional co-operation in order to mask the needs of a few private interests.

Formal regionalism in southern Africa, advocating liberalisation and privatisation, is promoted by an informal but nevertheless strong coalition of political and economic elite interests, led by Mbeki's government and his allies in the private sector (see Taylor, 2001). This tends to draw in elites from the neighbouring countries as well as external and "global" interests. Certainly, open regionalism and regional state-business partnerships are strongly supported by the IFIs and American and European donor agencies (Söderbaum, 2002). The historical irony is that this resembles colonial capitalism with little or no direct concern for the people on the ground (i.e. the colonised). This fundamental problem undermines the MDC as a development corridor of real—rather than rhetorical—potential and makes us pessimistic regarding the overall potential of the "really existing" MDC as a model of development in southern Africa.

Crucially, one of the findings drawn out from this volume is that there can be an uneasy relationship between micro-regionalism and macro-regionalism. In fact, the two may contradict one another, or certainly stimulate processes and implies that undermine aspects of one or the other. Micro-regionalism, as we have noted, is connected to macro-regionalism in the way that broader regionalisation (and globalisation) energies produce potential for smaller and more economically active sub-national spaces to obtain immediate access to the larger regional economic complex. This may, particularly if the neo-liberal model is pursued, bypass the local national state and even national capital, in favour of transnational linkages. As the MDC demonstrates, such micro-regional processes may emerge as an alternative construction to the formal state-led regionalist project. Indeed, the type of "on the ground" process found in the MDC micro-region—customs evasion, smuggling, the evacuation of an effective form of state surveillance, the elevation of capital over and beyond the national administration—undermines both the state at the national level, but also calls into question the compatibility of the MDC micro-regional project with the wider SADC vision of a developmentally-oriented southern Africa moving ahead as one. Divergent processes stimulated by the MDC have been shown to create asymmetrical relations at a whole host of levels, deepening uneven development and sparking what may in some ways be regarded as a crisis in governance. Thus micro-regions and broader macro-regions are, if the MDC is anything to go by, uneasy bedfellows which may hold within them both powerful contradictions and the potential for destabilisation of any wider regional "vision". How this scenario may play out in the future micro-region around Maputo, and the larger southern African cone will likely bedevil the MDC and the SADC in years to come.

Bibliography

Abrahamsson, H. and Nilsson, A. (1995), *Mozambique: The Troubled Transition—From Socialist Construction to Free Market Capitalism*, London: Zed Books.

Adler, E. and Barnett, M. (eds) (1998), *Security Communities*, Cambridge: Cambridge University Press.

Amin, A. (1998), *An Institutionalist Perspective on Regional Economic Development*, paper prepared for the OECD Conference on Regional Development, Borås, Sweden, 29 January.

Arkwright, D., De Beer, G. and Mmatli, R. (1998), 'Spatial Development Initiatives in South Africa—Progress Achieved and Future Objectives', paper presented at *SAPES Trust Annual Colloquium*, Harare, September.

Asante, S.K.B. (1997), *Regionalism and Africa's Development. Expectations, Reality and Challenges*, Basingstoke: Macmillan.

Bach, D.C. (1999), *Regionalisation in Africa. Integration & Disintegration*, London: James Currey.

Bell, T. (1993), 'Should South Africa Further Liberalise its Foreign Trade', in M. Lipton and C. Simkins (eds), *State and Market in Post Apartheid South Africa*, Boulder: Westview Press.

Bernstein, H. (1998), 'Comments from Henry Bernstein' in 'Seminar on Spatial Development Initiatives in South Africa and Southern Africa: a summary of the proceedings', held at ETC UK 117 Norfolk Street North Shields Tyneside. 19 June.

Black, A. (1993), 'The Role of the State in Promoting Industrialization', in M. Lipton and Simkins, C. (eds), *State and Market in Post-Apartheid South Africa*, Boulder: Westview Press.

Bond, P. (2000), *Elite Transition: From Apartheid to Neoliberalism in South Africa*, London: Pluto Press.

Breslin, S. and Higgott, R. (2000), 'Studying Regions: Learning from the Old, Constructing the New', *New Political Economy*, vol. 5, no. 3 (November), pp. 333-352.

Breslin, S. and Hook, G. (eds) (2002), *Microregionalism and World Order*, Basingstoke: Palgrave.

BusinessMap (2000), *SADC Investor Survey. Complex Terrain*, A BusinessMap SA Report, Johannesburg: BusinessMap.

Bøås, M., Marchand, M. H. and Shaw, T. M. (eds) (1999), *New Regionalisms in the New Millennium*. Special Issue of *Third World Quarterly*, vol. 20, no. 5 (October).

Cahen, M. (1993), 'Check on Socialism in Mozambique—What Check? What Socialism?', *Review of African Political Economy*, vol. 20, no. 57. pp. 46-59.

Cerny, P. (1997), 'Paradoxes of the Competition State: The Dynamics of Political Globalisation', *Government and Opposition*, vol. 32, no. 2.

Cheru, F. (1997), 'Global *Apartheid* and the Challenge to Civil Society: Africa in the Transformation of World Order', in R. Cox (ed), *The New Realism: Perspectives on Multilateralism and World Order*, Basingstoke: Macmillan.

Christiansen, T. (2001), 'European and Regional Integration', in J. Baylis and S. Smith (eds), *The Globalization of World Politics: An Introduction to International Relations*, Oxford: Oxford University Press.

Clark, N. (1994), *Manufacturing Apartheid*, New Haven: Yale University Press.

Cox, R. (1996a), *Approaches to World Order*, Cambridge: Cambridge University Press.

Cox, R. (1996b), 'Global Perestroika' in R. Cox, *Approaches to World Order*, Cambridge: Cambridge University Press.

Cravinho, J. (1998), 'Frelimo and the Politics of Agricultural Marketing in Mozambique', *Journal of Southern African Studies*, vol. 24, no. 1, pp. 93-114.

Crush, J. (1997), 'Contract Migration to South Africa: Past, Present and Future', paper for the Green Paper Task Group in International Migration, Cape Town, January 13-14.

Davies, R. (2000), 'Building a New Relationship in Southern Africa: The Challenge Facing South Africa's Government of National Unity' in B. Hettne, A. Inotai and O. Sunkel (eds), *National Perspectives on the New Regionalism in the South*, Basingstoke: Macmillan.

De Beer, G. *et al.* (1999), 'The Future of the South African Borderlands', Pretoria: SDI.

De Melo, J. and Panagariya, A. (eds) (1993), *New Dimensions in Regional Integration*, Cambridge: Cambridge University Press.

Dieter, H., Lamb, G. and Melber, H. (2001), 'Prospects for Regional Cooperation in Southern Africa', in *Regionalism and Regional Integration in Africa: A debate of Current Aspects and Issues*, Discussion Paper 11, Uppsala: Nordiska Afrikainstitutet.

Driver, A. and De Barros, J. G. (2000), 'The Impact of the Maputo Development Corridor on Freight Flows', *DPRU Working Paper 00/38*, Cape Town: Development Policy Research Unit, UCT.

Du Toit, P. (1999), 'Peacebuilding in Africa: Prospects for Security and Democracy Beyond the State', *African Security Review*, vol. 8, no. 1.

Emmett, T. (2000), 'Beyond Community Participation? Alternative Routes to Civil Engagement and Development in South Africa', *Development Southern Africa*, vol. 17, no. 4, pp. 501-518.

Evans, P. (1996), 'Introduction: Development Strategies Across the Public-Private Divide', *World Development*, vol. 24, no. 6, pp. 1033-37.

Fawcett, L. and Hurrell, A. (eds) (1995), *Regionalism in World Politics. Regional Organization and International Order*, Oxford: Oxford University Press.

Frankel, S. H. (1938), *Capital Investment in Africa: Its Courses and Effects*, London: Oxford University Press.

Fukuyama, F. (1992), *The End of History and the Last Man*, New York: Free Press.

Gamble, A. and Payne, A. (eds) (1996a), *Regionalism and World Order*, Basingstoke: Macmillan.

Garrett, G. (1996), 'Capital Mobility, Trade, and the Domestic Politics of Economic Policy' in R. Keohane and H. Milner (eds), *Internationalization and Domestic Politics*, New York: Cambridge University Press.

Gibb, R. (1997), 'Regional Integration in Post-Apartheid Southern Africa: The Case of Renegotiating the Southern Africa Customs Union', *Journal of Southern Africa Studies*, vol. 23, pp. 67-86.

Grant, A. and Söderbaum, F. (2003), *The New Regionalism in Africa*, Aldershot: Ashgate.

Hall, P. V. (1998), 'Regional Institutional Structure and Industrial Strategy: Richards Bay and the Spatial Development Initiatives', paper presented at the *ACSP Conference*, Pasadena, California, 5-8 November.

Hanlon, J. (1991), *Mozambique: Who Calls the Shots?*, Oxford: James Currey.

Hanlon, J. (1996), *Peace Without Profit: How the IMF Blocks Rebuilding in Mozambique*, Oxford: James Currey.

Hanlon, J. (1999), 'Mozambique Notes', *Southern Africa Report*, vol. 14, no. 4, pp. 8-9.

Harrison, G. (1999), 'Corruption as "Boundary Politics": The State, Democratization, and Mozambique's Unstable Liberalization', *Third World Quarterly*, vol. 20, pp. 537-550.

Harrison, P. and Todes, A. (2001), 'The Use of Spatial Frameworks in Regional Development in South Africa', *Regional Studies*, vol. 35, pp. 65-85.

Hatty, P. R. (1993), 'The South African Trade Policy Debate: A Business Perspective', in P. Baker *et al.* (eds), *South Africa and the World Economy in the 1990s*, Cape Town: David Philip.

Held, D., McGrew, A., Goldblatt, D. and Perraton, J. (1999), *Global Transformations: Politics, Economics and Culture*, Cambridge: Polity Press.

Hentz, J. (1999), 'Regional Hegemony in Southern Africa', in W. F. K. Wambalaba (ed), *Dimensions of Contemporary African Development Strategies*, Dubuqe, IO: Kendall/Hunt.

Hentz, J. (2000a), 'Privatisation in Transitional South Africa', *Journal of Modern African Studies*, vol. 38, pp. 163-202.

Hentz, J. (2000b), 'QWERTY Worlds and South Africa's Preference Formation: Ideas and Policy-Making in Transitional South Africa', in S. Page (ed), *Regions and Development: Politics, Security and Development*, London: Frank Cass.

Hentz, J. (2002), 'The New Regionalism: Beyond Globalization', *Cooperation and Conflict*, vol. 37, pp. 350-6.

Hentz, J. and Hansen, M. (1999), 'Neo-colonialism and Neo-liberalism in South Africa and Zambia', *Political Science Quarterly*, vol. 114, pp. 479-502.

Hettne, B. (1993), 'Neo-Mercantilism: The Pursuit of Regionness', *Cooperation and Conflict*, vol. 28, no. 3.

Hettne, B. (ed) (1995), *International Political Economy. Understanding Global Disorder*, London: Zed Books.

Hettne, B. (1999), 'Globalization and the New Regionalism: The Second Great Transformation', in B. Hettne, A. Inotai and O. Sunkel (eds), *Globalism and the New Regionalism*, Basingstoke: Macmillan.

Hettne, B. (2002), 'The New Regionalism Revisited', in F. Söderbaum and T. M. Shaw (eds), *Theories of New Regionalism: A Palgrave Reader*, Basingstoke: Palgrave.

Hettne, B., Inotai, A. and Sunkel, O. (eds) (1999), *Globalism and the New Regionalism*, Basingstoke: Macmillan.

Hettne, B., Inotai, A., and Sunkel, O. (eds) (2000a), *National Perspectives on the New Regionalism in the North*, Basingstoke: Macmillan.

Hettne, B., Inotai, A., and Sunkel, O. (eds) (2000b), *National Perspectives on the New Regionalism in the South*, Basingstoke: Macmillan.

Hettne, B., Inotai, A., and Sunkel, O. (eds) (2000c), *The New Regionalism and the Future of Security and Development*, Basingstoke: Macmillan.

Hettne, B., Inotai, A., and Sunkel, O. (eds) (2001), *Comparing Regionalisms: Implications for Global Development*, Basingstoke: Palgrave.

Hettne, B. and Söderbaum, F. (eds) (1998), *The New Regionalism*. Special Issue of *Politeia*, vol. 17, no. 3.

Hettne, B. and Söderbaum, F. (2000), 'Theorising the Rise of Regionness', *New Political Economy*, vol. 5, no. 3, pp. 457-474 (November).

Hirsch, A. (1993), *Trading Up: Towards a Trade Policy for Industrial Growth in South Africa - Industrial Strategy Project Draft Final Report*, Cape Town, Development Policy Research Unit (DPRU), University of Cape Town.

Hirschman, A. (1981), *Essays in Trespassing: Economics to Politics and Beyond*, Cambridge: Cambridge University Press.

Hoogvelt, A. (1997), *Globalisation and the Post-colonial World: The New Political Economy of Development*, London: Macmillan.

Hook, G. and Kearns, I. (eds) (1999), *Subregionalism and World Order*, Basingstoke: Macmillan.

Hveem, H. (2000), 'Explaining the Regional Phenomenon in an Era of Globalization', in R. Stubbs and G. R. D. Underhill (eds), *Political Economy and the Changing Global Order*, Oxford: Oxford University Press (2nd Edition).

Ismail, F. and Jourdan, P. (1998), 'Comments from Faizel Ismail and Paul Jourdan' in 'Seminar on Spatial Development Initiatives in South Africa and Southern Africa: a summary of the proceedings', held at ETC UK 117 Norfolk Street North Shields Tyneside. 19 June.

Joffe, A, Kaplan, D., Kaplinsky, R. and Lewis, D. (1993), 'Meeting the Global Challenge: A Framework for Industrial Revival in South Africa', in P. Baker, A. Boraine and W. Krafchik (eds), *South Africa and the World Economy in the 1990s*, Washington, D.C.: The Brookings Institution.

Jourdan, P. (1998), 'Spatial Development Initiatives (SDIs): the Official View', *Development Southern Africa*, vol. 15, no. 5, pp. 717-25.

Jourdan, P., Gordhan, K., Arkwright, D. and De Beer, G. (1996), 'Spatial Development Initiatives (development corridors): Their Potential Contribution to Investment and Employment Creation', *SDI Policy paper*, SDI Unit: Midrand.

Katzenellenbogen, S. (1982), *South Africa and Southern Mozambique: Labour, Railways and Trade in the Making of a Relationship*, Manchester: Manchester University Press.

Kearns, I. and Hook, G. (1999), 'Conclusion: Subregionalism—an Assessment', in G. Hook and I. Kearns (eds), *Subregionalism and World Order*, Basingstoke: Macmillan.

Keating, M. and Loughlin, J. (eds) (1997), *The Political Economy of Regionalism*, London: Frank Cass.

Klak, T. and Myers, G. (1997), 'The Discursive Tactics of Neoliberal Development in Small Third World Countries', *Geoforum*, vol. 28, no. 2, pp. 133-150.

Koelble, T. (1998), *The Global Economy and Democracy in South Africa*, New Brunswick: Rutgers University Press.

Kritzinger-van Niekerk, L. (ed) (1997), *Toward Strengthening Multisectoral Linkages in SADC*, Midrand: DBSA.

Kyle, S. (1991), 'Economic Reform and Armed Conflict in Mozambique', *World Development*, vol. 19, no. 6, pp. 637-649.

Legum, C. (2000), 'Balance of Power in Southern Africa', in Y. Bradshaw and S. N. Ndegwa (eds), *The Uncertain Promise of Southern Africa*, Bloomington: Indiana University Press, pp. 12-26.

Leigland, J. and Thomas, R. (1999), 'The Need for an Integrated Approach to Market-Based Municipal Finance', *Development Southern Africa*, vol. 16, no. 4 (Summer).

Lewis, D. and Bloch, R. (1998), 'SDIs: Infrastructure, Agglomeration and the Region in Industrial Policy', *Development Southern Africa*, vol. 15, no. 5, pp. 727-69.

Lewis, S. (1990), *The Economics of Apartheid*, New York, Council on Foreign Relations.

Little, P. and Lundin, I. (1993), 'Trading to Eat: Petty Trade and Income Strategies in the Peri-urban Areas of Maputo, Mozambique', *Development Anthropology Network*, vol. 11, no. 2, pp. 1-8.

Maasdorp, G. G. (1994), *A Vision for Economic Integration and Cooperation in Southern Africa*, Pretoria, Department of Trade and Industry.

Maasdorp, G. G. (1996), 'Can Regional Integration Help Southern Africa?', in G. G. Maasdorp (ed), *Can South and Southern Africa become Globally Competitive Economies*, New York: St. Martin's Press.

Maasdorp, G. G. and Whiteside, A. (1993), *Rethinking Economic Cooperation in Southern Africa: Trade and Investment*, Johannesburg: Konrad-Adenauer Stiftung.

MacLeod, F. (2001), 'Vilanculos Coastal Wildlife Sanctuary', *Mail and Guardian*, 7 September 2001.

Mamdani, M. (1996), *Citizen and Subject: Contemporary Africa and the Legacy of late Colonialism*, Cape Town: UCT Press.

Mandaza, I. and Tostensen, A. (1994), *Southern Africa: In Search of a Common Future*, Gaborone: SADC.

Mansfield, E. D. and Milner, H. V. (eds) (1997), *The Political Economy of Regionalism*, New York: Colombia University Press.

Marais, H. (1998), *South Africa Limits to Change: The Political Economy of Transformation*, London: Zed Books.

Mattli, W. (1999), *The Logic of Regional Integration. Europe and Beyond*, Cambridge: Cambridge University Press.

McCarthy, C. (1992), 'South Africa as a Co-operative Partner in Southern African Trade and Investment', *Regional Economic Integration Conference*, Harare, Southern Africa Foundation for Economic Research, 3-4 December.

McGregor, J. (1994), 'People Without Fathers: Mozambicans in Swaziland, 1988-1993', *Journal of Southern African Studies*, vol. 20, no. 4, pp. 545-567.

McGregor, J. (1998), 'Violence and Social Change in a Border Economy: War in the Maputo Hinterland, 1984-1992', *Journal of Southern African Studies*, vol. 24, no. 1, pp. 37-60.

Midgley, J. (ed), (1986), *Community Participation, Social Development and the State*, London: Methuen.

Mistry, P. S. (2000), 'Africa's Record of Regional Cooperation and Integration', *African Affairs*, no. 99, pp. 553-573.

Mitchell, J. (1998), 'The Maputo Corridor: A Case Study of the SDI Process in Mpumalanga', *Development Southern Africa*, vol 15, no. 5, pp. 757-769.

Mittelman, J. H. (1996), 'Rethinking the New Regionalism', *Global Governance*, vol. 2, pp. 189-214.

Mittelman, J. H. (1999), 'Rethinking the New Regionalism in the Context of Globalization', in B. Hettne, A. Inotai and O. Sunkel (eds), *Globalism and the New Regionalism*, Basingstoke:.Macmillan.

Mittelman, J. H. (2000), *The Globalization Syndrome: Transformation and Resistance*, Princeton: Princeton University Press.

Mittelman, J. H. (2001), 'Subregional Responses to Globalization' in B. Hettne, A. Inotai and O. Sunkel (eds), *Comparing Regionalisms: Implications for Global Development*, Basingstoke: Palgrave.

Moloi, D. (1998), 'There's Logic in SDIs, But...', *Land and Rural Digest*, vol. 1, no. 1, June/July.

Mondlane, E. (1969), *The Struggle for Mozambique*, Harmondsworth: Penguin.

Mudenda, G. (2000), 'Cross-border White Farmer Migrations in Southern Africa: The Zambian Experience', in D. S. Tevera and S. Moyo (eds), *Environmental Security in Southern Africa*, Harare: SAPES Books.

Murphy, C. N. and Tooze, R. (eds) (1991), *The New International Political Economy*, Boulder: Lynne Rienner.

Murray, M. (1994), *The Revolution Deferred: The Painful Birth of Post-Apartheid South Africa*, London: Verso.

Nattrass, N. (1990), 'Economic Power and Profits in Post-war Manufacturing' in N. Nattrass and E. Ardington (eds), *The Political Economy of South Africa*, Cape Town: Oxford University Press.

Nel, E. (2002), 'South Africa's Manufacturing Economy: Problems and Performance', in A. Lemon and C. Rogerson (eds), *Geography and Economy in South Africa and its Neighbours*, Aldershot: Ashgate.

Neumann, I. B. (1999), *Uses of the Other. The East in European Identity formation*, Manchester: Manchester University Press.

Niemann, M. (1998), 'Regional Labour Migration in Post-apartheid Southern Africa', paper presented at the workshop 'Globalisms and regionalisms' of the IPSA study group III, New World Orders? University of Oslo, 6-8 August, 1998.

Nkuhlu, M. (1997), 'South Africa's Trade Policy with the SADC and Africa', in R. Hougton (ed), *Trading on Development: Proceedings of a Workshop on South Africa's Trade and Development Relations with the European Union*, Johannesburg: Foundation for Global Dialogue.

Odén, B. (2000), 'The Southern Africa Region and the Regional Hegemon', in B. Hettne, A. Inotai and O. Sunkel (eds), *National Perspectives on the New Regionalism in the South*, Basingstoke: Macmillan.

Osborn, E. (1992), 'Industrialisation, Liberalisation and Export Promotion', *Nedbank Quarterly Guide to the Economy*.

Oyejide, A. (1998), 'Trade Policy and Regional Integration in the Development Context: Emerging Patterns, Issues and Lessons for Sub-Saharan Africa', *Journal of African Economies*, vol. 7, Supplement 1, pp. 108-145.

Pagel, C. A. (1992), 'Areas of Competitive Advantage in South African Manufacturing', Masters dissertation: Rand Afrikaans University, November.

Penvenne, J. M. (1995), *African Workers and Colonial Racism: Mozambican Strategies and Struggles in Lourenço Marques, 1877-1962*, Portsmouth: Heinemann.

Perkmann, M. and Sum, N-G. (eds) (2002), *Globalization, Regionalization and Cross-Border Regions*, Basingstoke: Palgrave.

Pitcher, M.A. (1996), 'Recreating Colonialism or Reconstructing the State? Privatisation and Politics in Mozambique', *Journal of Southern African Studies*, vol. 22, pp. 49-74.

Poku, N. (ed) (2001), *Security and Development in Southern Africa*, Westport, CT: Praeger Publishers.

Prakash, A. and Hart, J.A. (1999), 'Globalization and Governance: An Introduction', in A. Prakash and J.A. Hart (eds), *Globalization and Governance*, New York: Routledge.

Rodolfo, B. (1998), 'Adjustment, Social Policy and Poverty in a War-torn Economy', *Southern African Political and Economic Monthly*, vol. 11, no. 8, p. 11.

Rodrik, D. (1997), *Has Globalization Gone Too Far?*, Washington, D.C.: Institute for International Economics.

Rogerson, C. (1998), 'Investment-led Entrepreneurship Development', *Development Southern Africa*, vol. 15, no. 5, pp. 917-41.

Rosenau, J. (1997), *Along the Domestic-Foreign Frontier: Exploring Governance in a Turbulent World*, Cambridge: Cambridge University Press.

Rostow, W. W. (1971), *Politics and Stages of Growth*. New York: Cambridge University Press.

Samatar, A. (1999), *An African Miracle: State and Class Leadership and Colonial Legacy in Botswana's Development*, Portsmouth: Heinemann.

Schulz, M., Söderbaum, F. and Öjendal, J. (eds) (2001), *Regionalization in a Globalizing World. A Comparative Perspective on Actors, Forms and Processes*, London: Zed Books.

Shaw, T. (2000), 'New Regionalism in Africa in the New Millennium: Comparative Perspectives on Renaissance, Realism and/or Regressions', *New Political Economy*, vol. 5, no. 3, pp. 399-414.

Shaw, T. (2003), 'Towards a Political Economy of Regional Conflict and Cooperation in Middle Africa at the Start of the Twenty-first Century', in J. Hentz and M. Bøås (eds), *New and Critical Security and Regionalism*, Aldershot: Ashgate.

Shaw, T.M. (2000), 'Africa in the Global Political Economy: Globalization, Regionalization, or Marginalization', in B. Hettne, A. Inotai and O. Sunkel (eds), *The New Regionalism*, Basingstoke: Palgrave.

Sidaway, J. (1993), 'Urban and Regional Planning in post-independence Mozambique', *International Journal of Urban and Regional Research*, vol. 17, no. 2, pp. 241-259.

Simon, D. (ed) (1998), *Reconfiguring the Region. South Africa in Southern Africa*, Oxford: James Currey.

Simpson, M. (1993), 'Foreign and Domestic Factors in the Transformation of Frelimo', *Journal of Modern African Studies*, vol. 31, pp. 309-337.

Smith, A. (1991), 'The Idea of Mozambique and its Enemies, c. 1890-1930', *Journal of Southern African Studies*, vol. 17, no. 3, pp. 496-524.

Stadler, A. (1987), *The Political Economy of Modern South Africa*, Cape Town: David Philip.

Söderbaum, F. (2002), *The Political Economy of Regionalism in Southern Africa*, PhD thesis, Göteborg: Padrigu.

Söderbaum, F. (2003), 'Regionalism', in N. Philips (ed), *The Globalisation of International Political Economy*, Basingstoke: Palgrave (in press).

Söderbaum, F. and Shaw. T. M. (eds.) (2003), *Theories of New Regionalisms. A Palgrave Reader*, Basingstoke: Palgrave.

Söderbaum, F. and Taylor, I. (2001), 'Transmission Belt for Transnational Capital or Facilitator for Development? Problematising the Role of the State in the Maputo Development Corridor', *Journal of Modern African Studies*, vol. 39, no. 4, pp. 675-95.

Taylor, I. (2000), 'The Maputo-Witbank Toll Road: Lessons for Development Corridors?', *DPRU Policy Brief Number 00/P5*, University of Cape Town.

Taylor, I. (2001), *Stuck in Middle GEAR: South Africa's Post-Apartheid Foreign Relations*, Westport: Praeger.

Taylor, I. (2002), 'The Maputo Development Corridor: Whose Corridor? Whose Development?' in S. Breslin, and G. Hook (eds), *Micro-Regionalism and World Order*, Basingstoke: Palgrave.

Tessely, R. (2001), 'Economic, Social and Political/Institutional Assessment of Spatial Development Initiatives', Masters Thesis, Department of Political Science, University of Stellenbosch.

Tevera, D. S. and Chimhowu, A. O. (2000), 'Spatial Development Initiatives and Regional Integration in Southern Africa', in D. S. Tevera and S. Moyo (eds), *Environmental Security in Southern Africa*, Harare: SAPES Books.

Thompson, C. (1992), 'African Initiatives for Development: The Practice of Regional Economic Cooperation in Southern Africa', *Journal of International Affairs*, vol. 46, pp. 125-44.

Torp, J. E. and Rekve, P. (1998), 'Privatisation in Developing Countries: Lessons to be Learned from the Mozambican Case', *Transformation*, vol. 36, pp. 73-92.

Tostensen, A. (1993), 'What Role for SADC(C) in the Post-Apartheid Era?', in B. Odén (ed), *Southern Africa after Apartheid*, Uppsala: The Scandinavian Institute of African Studies.

Tsie, B. (1996), 'States and Markets in Southern African Development Community: Beyond the Neo-liberal Paradigm', *Journal of Southern African Studies*, vol. 22, no. 1, pp. 75-98.

Van den Berg, J. (1987), 'A Peasant Form of Production: Wage-Dependent Agriculture in Southern Mozambique', *Canadian Journal of African Studies*, vol. 21, no. 3, pp. 375-389.

Van Zuydam, J. (1998), *Population Trends and Industrial Strategies in South Africa*, Proceedings of the Joint IASS/IAOS Conference in South Africa, Mexico City.

Venter, D. (1995), 'South Africa and Southern Africa. Towards a Symbiotic Relationship', *Africa Institute Bulletin*, vol. 1, no. 35, pp. 4-5.

Victorino, L. (2002), 'Cigarros e Bebidas Sujeitos à Revisão nas Importações' *Noticias–Economia e Negócios*, May 3.

Weeks, J. (1996), 'Regional Co-operation and Southern African Development', *Journal of Southern African Studies*, vol. 22, no. 1, pp. 99-117.

Weimer, B. (1996), 'Challenges to Democratization and Regional Development. Focus on Mozambique', *Regional Development Dialogue*, vol. 17, no. 2, pp. 32-59.

Williams, P. and Taylor, I. (2000), 'Neo-Liberalism and the Political Economy of the "New" South Africa', *New Political Economy*, vol. 5, no. 1.

Woods, N. (1999), 'Order, Globalization, and Inequality in World Politics', in A. Hurrell and N. Woods (eds), *Inequality, Globalization and World Politics*, New York: Oxford.

Reports and Documents

ADB (1992), *Economic Integration in Southern Africa: A Report for the African Development Bank*, mimeographed, Abidjan: African Development Bank.

DBSA (1997), *Interim Appraisal Report: Board Summary, Development Programme: Investment Project 10807—Witbank to Maputo Toll Road*, Halfway House: DBSA.

DBSA (1998a), 'Maputo Corridor Company Proposed Terms of Reference', <www.dbsa.org>.

DBSA (1998b), 'Spatial Development Initiatives and the Future Development of the South African Borderlands', <www.dbsa.org>.

DBSA (1998c), 'Planning Procedures for SDIs', <www.sdi.org.za> and <www.dbsa.org>.

DBSA (1999), 'Report to Cabinet Sub-Committee on Employment and Investment on Spatial Development Initiatives (SDI) Programme', Development Bank of Southern Africa: Halfway House.

DBSA (2001a), 'Development Perspective'. Development Bank of Southern Africa. <www.dbsa.org/Corridors/maputo/MaputoDevCorridor.htm>.

DBSA (2001b), 'Key Goals and Strategic Objectives for the Maputo Development Corridor', Development Bank of Southern Africa. <www.dbsa.org/Corridors/maputo/sectionc.htm>.

DBSA (2001c), 'Spatial Development Initiatives (SDIs) in Southern Africa', <www.dbsa.org>.

Department of Foreign Affairs (2000a), *The Economic Commission for Africa: Some Landmarks in the History of the ECA*, Pretoria: Directorate-OAU.

Department of Foreign Affairs (2000b), *The Economic Commission for Africa*, Pretoria: Directorate-OAU.

Department of Transport (1996), *White Paper on National Transport Policy*, Pretoria: Government Printers.

DTI (1998a), 'Seminar on Spatial Development Initiatives in South Africa and Southern Africa: a summary of the proceedings'. Held at ETC UK 117 Norfolk Street North Shields Tyneside. 19 June 1998.

DTI (1998b), 'Industrial Policy and Programmes in South Africa. A Discussion Document', Department of Trade and Industry, Pretoria.

ECA (1999), *The ECA and Africa: Accelerating a Continent's Development*, New York: Economic Commission for Africa.

ECA (2000a), 'Proposed Reform of the Intergovernmental Machinery of the Economic Commission for Africa', <www.un.org/Depts/eca>.

ECA (2000b), 'Serving Africa Better: Strategic Directions for the Economic Commission for Africa', <www.un.org/Depts/eca>.

Economist Intelligent Unit (2002), 'Country Report: Mozambique and Malawi', <www.store.eiu.com>.

GATT (1991), *Trade Policy Review, Vol. I*, Geneva, GATT.

GKG (2000), 'Plan for the Establishment of the Gaza-Kruger-Gonarezhou Transfrontier Park', <www.environment.gov.za/projprog/2000nov12/coneptplan.htm31/10/01>.

Harvard Business School (2000), 'Financing the Mozal Project', mimeographed.

IDC (1993), 'Competitive Advantage and the Promotion of Export Growth', Sandton: IDC.

IDC (2002), 'Impact of IDC Projects', presentation, Sandton, IDC, mimeographed. IFC (1997), *Annual Report*, <www.ifc.org/ar1997>.

IFC (2001), *Annual Report*, <www.ifc.org/ar2001>.

Industrial Strategy Project, (1993), 'Industrial Strategy Project', mimeographed.

SACOB (1993), *The Formulation of a New Industrial Policy for South Africa, discussion document*, Johannesburg, SACOB.

SADC (1993), Regional Relations and Cooperation: Post-Apartheid Southern Africa—A Macro Framework Study Report, Harare, SADC.

South African Consulate General (1990), 'Interdependence and Cooperation in Southern Africa', *South African Briefing Paper*, No. 3/90.

Internet Resources

ADB	www.afdb.org
ANC	www.anc.org.za
BusinessMap	www.businessmap.co.za
COMESA	www.comesa.int
COSATU	www.cosatu.org.za
DBSA	www.dbsa.org
DPRU	www.uct.ac.za/depts/dpru
Eskom	www.eskom.co.za
IDC	www.idc.org
MII	www.mii.co.za
Mozal	www.mozal.com
NEPAD	www.nepad.org
NUMSA	www.numsa.org.za
OAU/AU	www.au.org
SADC	www.sadc.int
SDI	www.sdi.org.za; www.africansdi.com
Spoornet	www.spoornet.co.za
TIPS	www.tips.org.za
UNECA	www.uneca.org
World Bank	worldbank.org
WTO	www.wto.org

Index

For Product Safety Concerns and Information please contact our EU representative GPSR@taylorandfrancis.com Taylor & Francis Verlag GmbH, Kaufingerstraße 24, 80331 München, Germany

Batch number: 10725923

Printed by Printforce, the Netherlands